something MORE

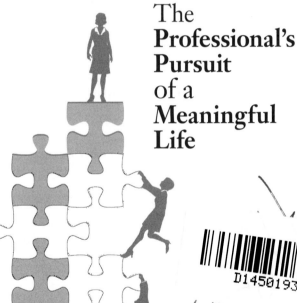

The
**Professional's
Pursuit**
of a
**Meaningful
Life**

D1450193

Liguori
LIGUORI, MISSOURI

Imprimi Potest:
Harry Grile, CSsR, Provincial
Denver Province, The Redemptorists

Published by Liguori Publications
Liguori, Missouri 63057

To order, call 800-325-9521
www.liguori.org

Cataloging-in-Publication Data on file with the Library of Congress

p ISBN 978-0-7648-2247-6
e ISBN 978-0-7648-2282-7

Liguori Publications, a nonprofit corporation, is an apostolate of The Redemptorists. To learn more about The Redemptorists, visit Redemptorists.com.

Printed in the United States of America
17 16 15 14 13 / 5 4 3 2 1
First Edition

What People Are Saying About
Something More

"Too many of us end up learning how to work efficiently but not effectively. Because of the demands on our personal and professional life, we play defense instead of offense with our time, energy, and resources. We just want to make it to Friday and hope that 'nobody gets hurt.' In this book, Randy Hain provides a road map to working and living on purpose. I highly recommend it to people who want to take control of their lives again."

> — **Dr. Tim Elmore**, author of *Artificial Maturity*,
> speaker, and president of GrowingLeaders.com

"About four decades ago, the cultural search began in our society for 'true happiness.' The next target was 'personal freedom.' That was followed by a wish for 'having it all.' Finally we were told that we should seek 'greater fulfillment.' Interestingly, none of those pursuits ever became fully realized because, as Randy Hain has shown us, the inherent virtue in all of them relies greatly on an individual's examination of self and on a determination to properly order our spiritual, personal, and professional endeavors. *Something More* guides the way."

> — **Allan J. DeNiro**, senior vice president and chief
> people officer of Haverty Furniture Companies,
> Inc., and author of *Failing Into Greatness*

"What has made my life meaningful is believing that, every day, God has a purpose for my life. I choose to embrace whatever that is and whomever he brings across my path. Randy's vast experience in working with a wide spectrum of people provides for a practical how-to book that teaches you to: recognize what's meaningful in the workplace for your particular purpose; implement God's specific plan for you; and courageously live a joy-filled life of purpose. If you didn't wonder if there wasn't more to life than your career, you wouldn't be holding this book now! There is. Start reading!"

> — **Susan O'Dwyer**, director of business
> development, Habif, Arogeti & Wynne, LLC

"Randy Hain continues to inspire. With this new book, we are reminded that we are universally created with a deep yearning for purpose and meaning. We seek to know that our life, our work, our relationships matter to the people around us. But integrated, authentic lives don't just happen. With Randy's help, through stories shared and insight given, we have the opportunity to choose 'intention,' and that intention coupled with grace will lead us to the gift of something more. A good read, an important book to share, and a great choice for a career-minded book study!"

— **Nancy Vepraskas**, president of P2Excellence,
a human capital consulting firm

"Randy Hain has done it again! As he did in his highly impactful book *Along the Way*, Hain takes the reader on a new journey of real-life challenges to find meaning and purpose in *Something More: The Professional's Pursuit of a Meaningful Life*. Hain challenges us in every chapter by weaving in stories and interviews of authentic people (including himself) who are challenged in professional settings to live a balanced life. Ultimately we relate and reflect on why we are where we are, how we got there, what is most important in our lives, and what we are going to do to achieve a life fulfilled. In *Something More*, Randy puts us on the right path."

— **Bob Howe**, founder and president,
CLICK 4 PAY, LLC

Contents

For my father, Steve Hain

Thank you for sharing your wisdom over the years and
for teaching me the value of a meaningful life.

Acknowledgments

*S*omething More: The Professional's Pursuit of a Meaningful Life is a labor of love written in response to an urgent need. Over my twenty-plus-year business career I have encountered thousands of professionals all over the country who have shared their desire to do something more with their lives than simply make a living. For those of you who have been willing to open up and candidly share what is on your mind and heart, I sincerely thank you. I wrote this book for you, me, and future generations who will one day arrive at a place in their lives where they desire to live more meaningful lives. I am hopeful this book will play a small part in helping all of us on our journey.

As I have shared in my previous books, no project like this is ever completed alone. I am grateful to the people of Liguori Publications for their enthusiastic support of the book and to my friend Lisa Tilt for her expert editing help, candor, and wise counsel.

I am blessed to have a circle of friends who each strive to lead meaningful lives and who inspire me in so many ways. Thank you to Deacon Mike Bickerstaff, Mark Butler, Price Harding, Dr. Ron Young, Amelia Fox, Terry Trout, Dr. Bill Thierfelder, Paige Barry, Tom Peterson, Susan O'Dwyer, Dan Stotz, Jim Reese, Alex Munoz, Lacey Lewis, David McCullough, Tom Bates, Monica Johnson, Dr. Tim Elmore, Jo Ann Herold, Allen McNeill, Kevin Lowry, Matt Swaim, Dr. Phil Thompson, Joe Zuniga, Deborah Wilson, Carol Chizzolin, and all the members of the Woodstock Business Conference group.

I am grateful for the encouragement and support of my business partners Todd Warshaw and Matt Tovrog, as well as the entire Bell Oaks team.

This book would not be possible without the valuable contributions of Nicole Siokis, Beth Valenta, Richard Smith, Glen Jackson, Dr. Paul Voss, Dr. Karen Steadman, Dr. Dirk Baxter, Dean Harbry, Brandon Smith, Kimberly Samon, Andrea Chilcote, Curt Johnson, Tim Tassopoulos, Stephanie Tamargo, Ellina Feldman, Karen Bennett, Mark Newton, Tami Heim, Andreas Widmer and Amy Balog. Their candid insights into the diverse ways they pursue meaningful lives make the book authentic and accessible. I am grateful to all of you.

Chester Elton has been a great source of encouragement from the beginning; I appreciate his support and the kind foreword he wrote for the book.

My parents, Steve and Sandi Hain, taught me the value of hard work, the importance of family, to love and serve God, and to help anyone in need. I am so thankful that I know what a meaningful life is because of the way they lived their lives. Mom, your warm smile is missed every day. Dad, thank you for never pretending to be anyone other than yourself and for sharing the power of that with me.

Thank you to my wife, Sandra, and our sons, Alex and Ryan. You inspire me, keep me humble and give me a sense of purpose when I go to work each day. I love you and would not have a meaningful life without you.

Foreword

As my father was nearing the end of his life, he was very clear with his five boys that he didn't want a sad funeral. "Sing no sad songs for me," he said. Instead, he wanted his memorial to be a celebration of his life. As he put it, "I was the luckiest guy I knew."

Indeed, John Dalton Elton had lived a charmed life. He married his one and only sweetheart, Irene Tanner, or Ikey, as he called her—and their romance lasted sixty-two years. He'd had five healthy sons who had married five wonderful women. He'd had dear friends and a rich extended family.

As my father reminisced during his last few days, what was note-worthy was what little time he spent talking about his forty-plus years in radio. He was a world-class broadcaster who had interviewed presidents and prime ministers, sports heroes, and movie stars; and yet to listen to him speak, his life's work had been as a father, husband, and friend—who just happened to be in radio on the side. For my brothers and me, it was the last and greatest lesson we learned from our father.

During the funeral, my father got his wish. We sang happy songs, told jokes, and laughed a lot. Yes, we cried too; after all, it *was* a funeral. But to a person we left uplifted; my father had lived his life the right way.

In this wonderful book, *Something More: The Professional's Pursuit of a Meaningful Life*, Randy Hain helps you prioritize what is most important in your life and put those priorities where they belong—front and center. It is so easy to get caught up in our work and building our careers. In fact, at the time of my father's funeral, I was working eighty-hour weeks and had spent almost 200 days of the previous year on the road. I began thinking of a new life before I left my father's service, and within a year I had formed my own company with my own values and own schedule.

It's time for all of us to figure out what really matters. Few of us spend enough time where it really matters, in living meaningful lives. Randy provides a road map to a better work life, a better home life, and heck, just a better life.

I am pleased to add my thoughts to this work because I am proud to have known Randy professionally for years now and count him as one of my friends. He has inspired me to be a better person, and I know he will do the same for you.

It's important to understand that Randy lives what he writes about. This isn't theory or conjecture for him. What he presents are methods he has used that have worked for him as a busy, successful executive, and they will work for you. Follow this advice and make your life what it should be—happier, healthier, and more meaningful.

When loved ones gather for your funeral (many, many years from now), my wish for you is that they will say you lived your life the right way and that you leave behind a legacy of love, service, and good works. There will be laughter and tears of joy, I have no doubt, but there will be no sad songs.

CHESTER ELTON
THE NEW YORK TIMES BEST-SELLING AUTHOR OF
THE CARROT PRINCIPLE AND *ALL IN*

Introduction

He Had a Great Career

All good books tell a story. What you are about to read in the "Introduction" is a fable of sorts about a man who had it all, yet he wasn't fulfilled. It is a story of misplaced priorities, wasted opportunities, heartbreak, forgiveness, love, and ultimately, redemption.

A familiar tale, perhaps, that goes like this:

The sun shone brightly that September morning as the brothers stood next to the grave of their late father. Just a few minutes before, they had been surrounded by family and their father's business friends and their ears filled with the kind words of Father Benton, their parish priest. The words of praise about their father's life left them feeling empty and uncomfortable as they stared at the coffin in the ground.

"I can only say this to you, but I don't know how I should feel right now," Mike declared to Greg as they walked back to their car. "Dad spent our entire lives on an airplane, chained to his office or playing golf with his buddies on the weekend. I feel like we didn't even know him. I know this sounds selfish, but I feel cheated!"

Greg put his hand on his brother's shoulder, "Come on, Mike! It wasn't that bad. Dad had a lot of responsibility. He took good care of the family, and we never lacked for anything. He would have been around more if he could."

"Greg, you have always defended him, even when you hurt as much as I did when he missed our baseball games and Cub Scout camping trips. He even missed your high school graduation because of business! What about Mom? How did she feel all those years? Did you see her sobbing

on Aunt Mary's shoulder during the funeral? I wonder what she is thinking about the future now that Dad is gone. We'd better get over to Aunt Mary's for the reception and look in on her."

The brothers were lost in their own conflicting thoughts as they got in the car and drove to their aunt's home. Sadness...regret...and perhaps a little bitterness dominated their emotions as they joined the large crowd inside. There were hugs and sympathetic comments from all, and quite a few people encouraged them not to be sad and instead celebrate their father's life...which only made things worse in light of their recent conversation.

Then they saw their mother, who beckoned them to join her in Aunt Mary's office upstairs.

"Boys, we need to talk and we haven't had much time for that since your father's heart attack. The last few days have been a blur for me and I can only imagine what this has been like for you."

Mike spoke first, "Mom, Greg and I have been trying to wrestle with all of this, and it is hard. Since we have been in college, we have been even more distant than usual from Dad, other than the occasional phone call and holiday visits home. I know everyone expects us to be crying right now, but we can't help but remember a father who seemed to care about his job more than us. Maybe that's not fair, but that is how I feel."

Tears welled up in her eyes as she hugged her sons and asked them to sit down. "I know how hard it was for you growing up, and I tried my best to compensate for your father's hectic life. Your dad was a good man and he felt he was doing the right things for our family. But there was a recent change in him you weren't aware of. Over the last few months, your father started going to Mass with me again. We also had a few short conversations recently about his desire to do things differently with the rest of his life, and I could tell he had a heavy heart. He was coming to some big decision points about his life. Here is something I found next to the computer in your dad's study the morning after he passed away. Greg, will you please read this aloud for us?"

Greg nervously took the pages from his mother's hand and saw a typed letter to him and his brother from their father. It was dated September 12th—the day before he was found dead of a heart attack on the running trail near his office. He began reading...

September 12, 2011

Dear Mike and Greg,

I look forward to seeing you both during your Thanksgiving break from school. I have never written you boys before, so this may appear a little strange to you. My intention is to share a few important things that have been on my mind lately and discuss them when we are all together again.

I have been reflecting a lot lately on my life and the kind of husband and father I have been. It is probably no surprise to you that I give myself a failing grade. I realize very clearly that I have not been there for you and your mother over the years. It is easy to justify and rationalize our actions, and I have done that for years. I convinced myself that our big house, nice cars, great vacations, and the lifestyle I provided for us was worth my slavish devotion to my career. I thought this justified all of my absences and the sacrifices I forced our family to make over the years. I now realize that I was wrong.

Your mother is a saint, and she deserved much more from me in our twenty-four years of marriage. I have always loved your mother very much, but I rarely told her and thought I was showing her my love by providing a great lifestyle. I was a fool, and I am committed to making it up to her. She has been the bedrock of our family, and you boys are who you are because of your mother's great influence.

Greg...Mike...I owe you a sincere apology for not being there over the years. I really mean it. I have come to realize that all the stuff we have is meaningless compared to the lost opportunities to be a meaningful part of your lives. I hope you will forgive me and give me another chance when we sit down at Thanksgiving.

I am hopeful that in the years ahead we will become closer—the way a family should be. I want to reconnect with my Catholic faith and experience the joy I have seen in your mother's eyes when she talks about her faith or attends Mass. Serving in the community and giving back to others is also high on my list of new priorities.

I want you to promise me something...Please learn from my example! Be a better father, husband, and steward than I was, and don't waste the years ahead of you. I wish someone had gotten my attention when I was much younger and helped me not waste the greatest years of my life. I hope to do that for you in the years ahead.

I have seen the light and I hope to make amends. Again, please find it in your hearts to forgive me.

I truly love you more than you can ever know.

Dad

There were tears streaming down all their faces. Greg and Mike hugged their mother as the anger and resentment they had felt gave way to genuine grief.

Mike spoke first, "I only wish we had time to have that Thanksgiving together...to truly get to know each other and start over. I would have liked to have known the man who wrote this letter."

Greg was clutching the pages tightly as he whispered, "We need to pray for Dad and that we will learn from his mistakes and pass these lessons on to our own children. It is strange that the thought occurred to me at the grave that his headstone should read 'He Had a Great Career,' and now I want it to say, 'Loving Father and Husband' to honor his last-minute conversion."

Their mother responded, "Boys, please don't wait until the end of your lives to make amends. I have no doubt that your father would have done what he said, but you can't wait like he did. Start living today like it is the last day of your lives."

— The End —

Some of us may know people like the father in the story and the unintentional misguided priorities they pursued in their lives. I know this character very well because...I am the father in this story. Let me explain (I'll go into more detail in the next chapter as well). In December of 1999, I left a very successful career as the vice president of recruiting for a national billion-dollar restaurant chain where I was responsible for the company's recruiting and diversity efforts, leading a team of fourteen people. As a thirty-two-year-old officer of the company, I had significant responsibility, the respect of my peers, and a bright future ahead of me. But as much as I loved the work, I was miserable.

I traveled three weeks a month for four years. I worked most weekends and put in around seventy to eighty hours a week. As a member of the leadership team, I was expected to be in the restaurants on every major holiday to set a good example. That does not mesh well with a young family. I saw my infant son growing up before my eyes and I was barely present. My wife and I were growing distant because of my workaholic tendencies and the demands of my job. I looked around me and saw many of my peers having marital problems or they were already divorced. I made a conscious decision to leave the organization and get my life back on track. I was being pursued at that time by my current company and was drawn to the opportunity and the work/life balance it offered. The great company culture and strong values of the leadership team were also very appealing. I made a decision to join the new company and shocked everyone who knew me. They thought I was committing career suicide, but I knew I was saving my family and embarking on the pursuit of a life filled with meaning. The years since have validated my decision in positive ways I could never have imagined.

Why did I write the title "He Had a Great Career?" I often wonder what would have happened if I had never left my old employer in 1999 and simply looked ahead twenty to twenty-five years. This tragic story could have easily been my own story if I had not made some critical decisions about work, family, faith, and life.

Throughout this book you will read not only my thoughts and observations, but those of many successful professional men and women from diverse backgrounds around the country who graciously agreed to be interviewed for the project. I was struck by two things in these interviews: (1) Every single person was passionate about pursuing a meaningful life, although that means something different for each of them and (2) with little overlap, each person I interviewed had varying motivations for aspiring to a meaningful life. These motivations typically revealed themselves after deep reflection on various questions such as: "Who am I?" "What do I want from life?" "What role does God play in my life?" "What is truly important to me?" "What am I good at?" and "What will be my legacy?"

My sincere hope is that you will find hope, encouragement, and helpful tools through my words and the stories of these men and women who have in their own ways made the all-important decision to pursue and achieve lives filled with purpose and meaning. We learn to make positive changes in our lives by emulating the good and virtuous behaviors we observe in others. This book is not about theory but about the practical pursuit of lives worth living. Each person introduced in the following pages has defined what this is in his or her own way, and each has taken a different path to arrive there, but from this eclectic mix of courageous business professionals you may find the tools you need and the path you are seeking to find your own meaningful life.

Author's Note: You will read frequent references in this book to community service and serving on nonprofit boards. In appendix one you will find a helpful guide titled *A Road Map for Effectively Serving on Nonprofit Boards* that should prove useful. Also, because so many professionals are dealing with the challenges of current or looming career transition, I have included a guide to dealing with a job search in an interesting way titled *The Upside of a Job Search in a Down Economy* (appendix two).

chapter
ONE
Something Is Missing

*"Ultimately I believe we seek more meaningful lives
in the hope of filling some emptiness
that exists within us."*

I begin with the assumption that you agree that a "meaningful life" is a very good thing. We all may define what this means a little differently, but in the end, it is lofty, noble, inspirational, and fulfilling to pursue this kind of life. In order to begin, some need a process or a road map to show the way. Some just need to get started and take a leap of faith. Truth be told: For many of us, the journey begins as a nagging feeling that something is missing in our lives. Maybe you can't quite put a finger on the problem or know for certain that the path you have been on no longer holds the same appeal. For some of us, we know what is missing and simply need help to find it and make it a part of our lives. Ultimately I believe we pursue more meaningful lives in the hope of filling some emptiness that exists within us.

For most of my career I have been working with candidates, clients, and other professionals who are seeking something more out of life. These professionals realize at different ages and stages of their careers that what they are seeking cannot be satisfied by their careers alone. They often talk of reinvesting in their marriages, spending more quality time with their children, developing stronger faith lives or giving back to the community. Sometimes they simply want to do the work they love and collect more than just a paycheck.

When I was a new college graduate, I thought of nothing more than going to work for a solid company and rising to the top. My parents had instilled a great work ethic in me as a teenager, and I was willing to work as hard as necessary to achieve my career goals. I was single-minded in my focus as I consistently worked insane hours at the national retail company I joined right out of school, and it paid off as I was given significant leadership and P & L responsibility at a relatively young age. Then I met my future wife…and my life would never be the same. But I found it difficult to change old habits.

As we fell in love and later got married, I recognized intellectually that my career alone would no longer suffice. I now had a wonderful partner in my life and something needed to give, but I found it challenging to abandon my workaholic tendencies and put our family first. To make matters worse, I made a significant career change shortly after we married to join the national billion-dollar restaurant company I mentioned in the "Introduction" and quickly rose to become the vice president of recruiting and an officer of the company by the time I was thirty-two years old. While the outside world would have rated my career successful, my life was dramatically out of balance and I knew I needed to change; but I wasn't sure where to begin.

During my time with this company our first son was born and, despite all of my career success, I felt like I was failing as a father and husband. I traveled more than eighty percent of the time for most of my four years with the organization and had difficulty turning work off when I was at home. My wife and newborn son were clearly getting what was left over from the time I gave my job.

Fortunately for me, an old boss of mine called at the beginning of my fourth year with the restaurant company and began trying to recruit me to his organization, which was a boutique national executive search firm. I was nervous and hesitant despite knowing I desperately needed a change for the sake of my family. Ego and pride played a part in my indecision as I considered the logic in leaving a billion-dollar organization for a company with less than five million dollars in revenue. I would be giving up a relatively secure and sizable income for a compensation plan based on salary and commission, but I decided to explore this opportunity further.

Before I began the interviews, I made a list of criteria that needed to be met before I would change careers. I felt I needed to be absolutely sure I was making the right decision for myself and my family, so I came up with the following list:

1. *The company needs to strongly support work/life balance.* It was vitally important that my workaholic tendencies would not be fed by the demands of the organization.
2. *The company leadership team needs to have strong values.* I wanted to work for an organization I respected and would be proud to represent.
3. *I needed an uncapped income opportunity.* I am not really financially motivated, but I wanted to provide comfortable living situations for my family and give my wife the opportunity to be a stay-at-home mom.
4. *I needed an intellectual challenge.* I needed a job that would stretch me and further my continued growth and development.

The leadership team impressed me, as did their stellar reputation in the business community. The more I interviewed with the organization, the more I felt like part of their family. After discussing it over at length with my wife, I joined the new company in December of 1999. I have been with Bell Oaks Executive Search ever since, running the company as managing partner for most of those years. With work/life balance established, my life was back on track. Or so I thought.

Sometimes life has a way of getting our attention. Our oldest son was diagnosed with autism at the age of twenty-seven months. We had noticed developmental delays over his first two years but never dreamed it was autism. My wife and I were devastated. We desperately needed help to sort out why this happened but didn't know where to turn. After a week of soul-searching and recognizing that this was about our son and not us, we threw ourselves into his care and have dedicated ourselves ever since to giving him the unconditional love he needs and all the support possible. Today our son is a teenager with high-functioning autism making great grades in school. He has social quirks and other challenges, but he is a true blessing in our lives, and we are hopeful that he will lead as independent a life as possible

The years passed in my new company, and our second son was born in 2001. Work had never been better, my marriage was thriving, and we had two wonderful sons we adored. I should have been content, but deep down I knew something was still missing. My previous notions of the missing piece being simply work/life balance had all but subsided; I sensed that the challenging period around our older son's autism diagnosis had awakened something in me that I couldn't identify. I felt restless and empty when I thought I should have been deliriously happy with the state of my life. Little did I know that everything was about to be turned upside down! In 2005 we decided to move from North Atlanta where we had lived for eleven years to a new home further south in another suburb of Atlanta that was closer to my office and our older son's therapists and school. All of that year I acutely felt I was coming to a crisis point in my life. Incidentally, this was the year I turned forty, and the restlessness I felt was increasingly a challenge for me. People who know me typically say I always have a game plan and that I am self-confident, but during the year leading up to the move I felt as if I was coming apart at the seams and I no longer had a plan for my life.

While my personal crisis was escalating, my wife was pursuing her own journey to fill a void in her life and was investigating the Catholic Church in which she had been baptized but never confirmed. She asked me to look into the Church with her and I agreed. Having no faith in my life since leaving the Baptist Church as a sixteen-year-old, I was hesitant; yet I knew on some level that I needed God back in my life. I investigated and was immediately drawn to the Catholic Church's history and tradition and hoped it would have answers for what was missing in my life. After a summer of study and a series of conversations with a priest at the parish near our home, we made the decision to join the Church. That nagging feeling that something was still missing after my work and family situation improved was actually a sincere longing for the Truth, and now I had found it. Making this decision that got me back on course with my life felt like Saul on the road to Damascus mixed with the prodigal son.

Since my conversion, I have striven to lead an integrated and meaningful life with a new list of priorities: Christ is first, family is second, and work is third. I have abandoned my old compartmentalized life for an integrated existence with my faith at the center of everything. My faith and newfound balance with work has opened the door to countless blessings for my family and my career. I lead a team of professionals who make me proud every day and I am actively involved in serving area nonprofits (see appendix two) and leading ministries in my parish. I have also developed a passion for writing and speaking over the last several years.

My experience may be quite different from yours, and I recognize that faith may not play as big a part for others as it did for me. I simply wanted to share a glimpse of my journey over the years so as to plant a seed of thought on why a "meaningful life" is so important and to encourage you to pursue one of your own. I was missing not only balance in my life, but faith as well. Later, with a strong faith and balance restored at home, another missing piece of the meaningful-life puzzle was revealed as I began writing, speaking, and more actively serving in the community. I feel very fortunate to have recognized what was missing from my life and know how critical this realization was in my pursuit of a life filled with purpose and meaning.

Questions for Reflection

◇ Do I feel like something is missing in my life and, if so,
do I know what it is?

◇ If I can address what is missing in my life,
how will I act differently?

◇ How have I dealt with balance problems over my career?

◇ As I address the question of what is missing in my life,
how much of this do I own (that is, choosing faith,
career change, altering my behaviors)? How much is
out of my control?

chapter
TWO
Knowing Our Motivations

*"...People rarely embark on the path to richer and
fuller lives without first recognizing on a
fundamental level what drives them."*

I was taught at a young age to work hard and excel at everything I do. I had great examples to follow in my parents. My growing faith, love for my family, and desire to provide security for them as well my desire for ongoing personal growth are the major motivations in my life. Being self-aware about this allows us to more accurately assess where we are in life and pursue what we want and where we want to go.

One professional who did this is Nicole Siokis. Nicole has a fascinating background as a former Army officer born in Germany to a military family. She met her husband, also an Army officer, and left the military to begin a successful corporate career with a national multibillion-dollar organization. With the birth of her daughter and a few years of soul-searching around the questions "Who am I?" "What is truly important to me?" and so on, she purchased a Mom Corps franchise for a major U.S. city and became the president of this regional business in 2009.

Nicole, how would you describe a "meaningful life?"

"We all find meaning in different ways throughout life. How we find meaning may even evolve as we continue our journey throughout our own lives. At the end of our journey, I believe we must be able to answer the question 'am I happy with how I lived my life?' For me, there must be a balance of the contributions I have made in other people's lives—family, friends, colleagues, and strangers—as well as my own personal growth. Am I doing the things that will leave behind a positive impact in the lives of others, in my community, and in the world in general?"

To many, a meaningful life is primarily all about finding balance. You obviously see it as much more than simply balance. What are the various components of a meaningful life from your own experience and from others in your life?

"As a parent, I wholeheartedly believe the most important thing to consider, in terms of a meaningful life, is—for me—the impact it has on my child. Not only is it important for me to be 'present' in my daughter's life—giving her the building blocks to be strong and confident—but to also set a good example that instills the fundamentals which make her a compassionate, selfless human being who contributes positively to the rest of the world. My daughter is part of the 'me' generation, so I believe it's important for her to understand it is not just about 'me,' but rather about 'us.'

"I also find that volunteering, particularly with organizations focused on helping girls and women, helps fulfill my need to contribute to a greater good. Many others I know find meaning from their faith and getting involved in a church.

"Lastly, I need to find meaning in the work I do. I am fortunate to own a business focused on helping businesses fill professional-level positions with smart, successful women who want to work but who also want to have the flexibility to lead a balanced life."

When did you recognize your own need to pursue a meaningful life? What was the catalyst for you?

"It was definitely when my daughter was born. As a parent, you have one chance to get it right. I no longer wanted to be consumed with work and realized there is a much bigger reason for everything I do. I also knew it was important to be a very positive role model for all the things she could do in her life and all the things she can be."

It took a lot of courage to walk away from your successful career to buy the Mom Corps franchise for Atlanta. What was your thinking process and motivation behind that decision?

"The answer to this question goes back to the point I made in the first question. My definition of a meaningful life has evolved as I have gotten older. I began my career in the military with aspirations to become a leader of a large organization. Then I met my husband. My father was in the military and I knew firsthand that military life can be hard. I decided to pursue a career in corporate America, with the same aspirations of becoming a successful leader of a large organization. Then I had my daughter and everything changed again. I knew that I wanted to work and contribute in a meaningful way, but I also knew I wanted to be a very active and involved mother.

"Like many women, I faced a tough challenge in an organization that offered little flexibility. When the Mom Corps opportunity ultimately presented itself, it felt like a natural fit with my passion for entrepreneurship partnered with the ability to work flexibly, which is a concept I strongly believe in. Owning and running the Mom Corps Atlanta franchise has been a blessing because of the wonderful opportunity we have given many people who are desperately seeking some sort of flexibility with work-life balance, a concept in which I strongly believe. It is also amazing to see how companies are evolving and embracing the concept of workplace flexibility as well."

What advice would you offer other professionals who may feel trapped in their jobs and who are longing to do more, give more, and achieve more in life?

"First, take time to really find out what is missing in your life and what you want and need to feel more fulfilled (that is, more volunteer time, more flex time, etc.). Second, seek out role models who do the things you want to do as well. Set up time to meet with people and learn what they do and how they make it work. If what you are looking for requires time away from work, prepare for a discussion with your boss and be prepared to offer alternative solutions based on the research you have done. Many companies are beginning to embrace flex time or volunteer time and do not necessarily expect a trade-off in work hours. Unfortunately, many employees are not even aware of these options until they ask."

Nicole, do you believe that pursuing a life filled with meaning and purpose is achievable for everyone? If so, what are the obstacles holding so many people back?

"I do actually. I think fear is the biggest deterrent ('nobody else has done this so I doubt they would make an exception for me' is an example of a work-related fear). I think it is also very easy for people to get caught up in the day-to-day and spend very little time reflecting inward. Some of the most successful people I know have developed a personal mission statement and actually schedule time, first thing in the morning or throughout the day, to reflect on the things they have done or plan to do and ask 'is this contributing to my personal mission statement?' It can be really hard to do, but once it becomes habit, it can keep you focused on the life you want to live."

There is much to appreciate about Nicole's transparency and the determination she has shown in pursuing a fuller and more meaningful life. It seems clear that being a great mother, her daughter's future, giving back to others, flexibility, and being an entrepreneur have been the primary motivators behind the career choices she has made.

What about you? What are your motivations? As I shared in chapter one, my motivations have been relatively consistent but evolving. From my experience, people rarely embark on the path to richer and fuller lives without first recognizing on a fundamental level what drives them. Please also realize that negative and unhealthy motivations can have a major influence on our decisions in life. Blind ambition, insecurity, greed, excessive pride, and fear of failure can all fall into the category of unhealthy drivers that can frustrate our desire to make good decisions that lead to a more meaningful life.

Questions for Reflection

◇ What are my motivations to lead a meaningful life?

◇ How does Nicole's example resonate with me? What are key lessons I can absorb from her choices?

◇ Do I have unhealthy motivations that are blocking me from my goals? What are they? What will I do to address them?

◇ What is my personal mission statement? How can I live it every day?

chapter
THREE
Assessing the Obstacles

*"Fear, frustration, self-doubt, lack of knowledge, lack of
self-awareness, stress, lack of boundaries, economic
conditions, illness—these are a few of the many
obstacles that can get in the way as we
pursue meaningful lives."*

A t this point, we not only know something is missing, but we also have a better grasp of the motivations behind our decisions. These are vital pieces of the life puzzle, but before we go too far down the path we have to address the obstacles that can get in our way. I have always been a firm believer in clearly understanding what can potentially keep us from achieving our goals. These derailers are a consistent theme with the professionals I encounter and certainly the people interviewed for this book. Identifying these obstacles and overcoming them is necessary if we hope to attain more meaningful lives.

As I researched the topic of this chapter, I sought out the insights of Dr. Karen Steadman and Dr. Dirk Baxter, both principals of Leadership Futures, a well-regarded national consulting and coaching firm. Because they work extensively with senior business leaders and their organizations on coaching, development, and employee engagement, I was curious to get their take on obstacles that often prevent their clients and employees from achieving more meaning in their lives.

As I know you both are heavily involved with a number of clients across the country from various industries, I am very curious about what you are observing and hearing from the business people you encounter each day.

Dr. Karen Steadman: "In our recent experience the coaching world has shifted. People are tired from difficult economic times and life that appears to be getting complex at an exponential rate. Modern day in corporate America may not have the significant difficulties comparable to war and famine; however there are lessons to be learned over what humans cherish even during the most difficult times—connections to close family and friends, humor and happiness, spirituality or something 'bigger' than themselves, and the beauty of nature [Frankl, Viktor (1946), *Man's Search for Meaning*, latest edition: Beacon Press, 2006]. Recent statistics reveal that conflicts between work and life commitments are increasing even in more traditional roles for men. In 2009, thirty-one percent of men revealed that they would welcome a reduced salary if it would help provide better balance between work and home activities. This number had been as high as fifty percent in 2005 before the recession, revealing that given the right circumstances employees want more than a paycheck (CareerBuilder.com, June 14, 2005: 'Nearly one-half of working dads would relinquish breadwinner role to spend more time with their kids, Annual Father's Day Survey.' And from CareerBuilder.com June 17, 2009: 'Fewer working fathers willing to be stay-at-home dads than previous years.')."

How are you achieving the best results for your clients in light of this observation? Do you connect your coaching to achieving a more meaningful life?

Dr. Dirk Baxter: "We've seen the best sustainable results when coaching our clients to put more effort into less—to hyper-focus their limited energy on the intersection between (1) skills and behaviors that are required to be successful within their unique organization and stakeholder group and (2) areas they willingly choose to change for reasons bigger than themselves. Helping clients find meaning in why it is worth changing is now included in 100 percent of the work we do because, honestly, the change doesn't seem to stick otherwise. Life is too complicated and the *status quo* is too compelling without the 'why' someone should change."

Do you ever sense that business people you encounter feel trapped in their careers? Can you share any relevant examples of how they overcome this challenge?

Dr. Karen Steadman: "The leaders we work with are results-driven, which has ultimately helped them be successful. However, as they move through levels of leadership they start to run out of options because they keep trying to use the same strategies and they are exhausted. It is suffocating for them and many feel trapped on a treadmill. Helping them choose areas and connecting to something meaningful provides freedom for change and excitement about evolving their skills and re-energizing their scope of effectiveness. For examples, the following leaders created action plans with tangible business impact targets yet also goals that had more meaning to them than merely 'driving results.'

— "A senior VP-operations of a Fortune 500 insurance company added 'find joy every day' and 'help clear a path for other women leaders' as her overarching reasons to build more collaborative relationships with her peers at work and modify her derailing competitive behaviors.

— "A VP-procurement for a Global 1000 stated, 'I want to improve my ability to influence at the strategic level because it will allow me to get my work done more effectively here, which means I can balance my life overall. I don't influence well and I end up working 24/7 because of it. This is no longer acceptable, as we have a young child at home and it isn't worth it anymore.'

— "A VP-quality in healthcare agreed that her lack of ability to set strong boundaries and have difficult conversations was impeding her ability to drive results. She summarized, stating, 'I am clearly not working in balance, and it isn't helping anyone, especially me. I'm not happy, and I now have some tangible actions I can take to be more effective for the team and be happier again.'

"Similarly, we've noticed a shift in stakeholders. Interviews with those who work most closely with the leader often reinforce similar messages and encourage leaders to achieve loftier and more meaningful goals. 'It will help all of us if he would just dial down the intensity,' quoted a stakeholder in speaking of a regional VP in retail. Our interviews often reveal underlying needs that aren't always specifically stated on leadership competency models but help drive better work and life behaviors. For examples, stakeholders often share feedback suggesting leaders should:

◇ "Reduce their intensity.
◇ "Improve the ability to pause and reflect.
◇ "Set better boundaries.
◇ "Increase resilience to stress.
◇ "Role model work/life balance.
◇ "Have more fun.
◇ "Do more 'people-oriented' things such as ask about families and children.
◇ "Take real vacations and don't send e-mails while they are away from work.
◇ "'Stay hydrated for the marathon.' In other words, create sustainable climates at work."

As you both reflect on your experiences, have you observed that what each person seeks in a meaningful life is unique, and is there a measurable upside for companies if their leaders overcome their obstacles to achieve it?

Dr. Dirk Baxter: "Without a doubt! One of the most expensive mistakes made in hiring and promotions occurs when aspirations are assumed rather than questioned (Martin, Jean & Schmidt, Conrad, 'How to Keep Your Top Talent,' Harvard Business Review, May 1, 2010). Similarly, there is no alternative for asking the question about what is meaningful as each person is unique. Whether it is more beauty, more happiness, a lasting legacy, or less insanity they seek—many leaders are taking responsibility to find balance and create climates that allow for flexibility. These leaders are reaping the rewards with more engaged employees as evidenced recently at a board meeting in Talkeetna, Alaska, when the CFO made the following comment, 'Mount McKinley hasn't looked this beautiful in the thirty-one years I have been here. I recommend we modify our agenda to make sure we all have a chance to take pictures.' We've never seen a team more effectively tackle their tasks in order to take advantage of what was a unique life experience bigger than themselves. Considering that organizations with engaged, enabled, and energized employees can produce greater than twenty-five percent annual operating margins, it is our recommendation that leaders lose their fear and do a better job of working toward and sharing what is meaningful to them. Their unspoken motivations of 'why' are likely more aligned with their organizations and their stakeholders than they might imagine."

Fear, frustration, self-doubt, lack of knowledge, lack of self-awareness, stress, lack of boundaries, economic conditions, illness—these are a few of the many obstacles that can get in the way as we pursue meaningful lives. The question is, will we remain where we are in light of these challenges or will we overcome them? For a different perspective on overcoming challenges, I reached out to businessman Mark Newton. I know Mark to be a devoted husband and father and man of strong faith. He is known in the nonprofit community of Atlanta as a generous steward of his gifts and knowledge. What many people don't know about Mark is that he founded a startup named irunurun while still heading up his structured-settlement consulting and insurance business that he started almost twenty years ago. Irunurun is an emerging software and professional services company whose mission is to help people achieve their potential in work and life.

Mark has long had an interest around accountability and efficiency and had a chance to marry these passions to the irunurun software product in January 2010. I caught up with Mark to discuss his pursuit of a life filled with meaning and the obstacles he overcame to make this dream a reality.

We have had a few conversations over the years about our shared desire to lead meaningful lives. Can you sum up in a nutshell what that means to you?

"That's easy! A life in which we work hard, serve others, and ultimately, live obediently before God."

You have shared with me before that we tend to place too much emphasis on work/life balance. What are the key components of a meaningful life from your own experience and from others you have observed?

"I believe balance is often misunderstood. I'm not sure anyone has ever achieved greatness through balance. Soldiers, athletes, presidents, missionaries all live unbalanced lives. To be great at what we do as business people and parents, we must at times strive more in one area of life than others. I think what is important is how we recover and the state of our relationships.

"For me, components to a meaningful life are a healthy focus on faith, family, and work. I really enjoy spending time with people who seem to have gotten all of these right."

Mark, is this idea of leading a life filled with meaning actually achievable? If so, what gets in the way of more people making this a reality?

"Absolutely. This life is short. Pray about it; seek wise counsel, and then move. Life won't be meaningful without real meaning. Three big obstacles to accomplishing this come to mind:

— "Fear: I once heard of a company that asks its employees what they would do if they were not afraid. Great question!

— "Being Overwhelmed: We live in the busiest society in history. E-mails, voicemails, texts, noise, etc., keep us numb to the dreams in our hearts. Back away. Listen. Act.

— "Lack of Discipline: My kids are getting older. Business is demanding. I'm more involved than ever in nonprofit work and church. I need the discipline to handle it all effectively. Listening and reflection are big right now."

It must have been difficult to walk away from actively leading your successful business to start a technology company. What was your thinking process behind that decision?

"It wasn't exactly what I wanted to do. I didn't want a distraction. For once in my career, I was focused. However, with strong prompting from business mentors, good friends and other key influencers in my life—coupled with confirmation through prayer—I knew it was right. As children came along and my responsibilities grew, I saw an ever-increasing need for this product. Irunurun stemmed from a desperate prayer, a prayer for help in what was at the time a struggling insurance practice."

Mark faced a number of obstacles in taking the leap of faith to found irunurun:

— Mark put his financial security at risk when he invested in and began devoting time to the new company.

— He dealt with the inherent challenges of getting a new-technology product to market.

— His own challenges around self-discipline were part of the reason he felt led to launch irunurun. Ironically, he overcame this major obstacle by starting the new company, which is focused on increasing productivity, efficiency, and results.

As you consider the obstacles in your life and the input from Dr. Steadman, Dr. Baxter, and Mark Newton, remember that you need a starting place, and learning self-awareness is what I recommend. If you are struggling to identify the obstacles holding you back, go to people who will tell you the truth versus what they think you want to hear and solicit their candid input and advice. It is a good rule of thumb to always keep people like this in your inner circle, as we are often unaware of (or unwilling to acknowledge) our own failings.

Questions for Reflection

◇ What obstacles are in the way of me leading a more meaningful life? Make a list.

◇ Which obstacles do I own? Which ones are seemingly out of my control? Develop a game plan to deal with both.

◇ Consider the interview with Dr. Steadman and Dr. Baxter. Do I feel trapped in my career and my life? If so, why?

◇ Who can I seek out for guidance to help me identify and address my obstacles? I will commit to picking someone who is direct, honest, and willing to tell me the truth.

chapter
FOUR
Recalibration

"...At some point the path to a meaningful life will lead to a crossroads, and difficult choices will often be required."

All of us have or will reach important decision points in our lives that will change how we view our careers. We will either recognize the need to make these changes or the change will be thrust upon us. The first three chapters have led us down the road toward our goal and perhaps we can even begin to see what it looks like off in the distance, but awareness is not enough. We have been trained by our culture and often our experiences to climb the corporate ladder and measure our success in terms of income, possessions, and career achievement. If we want to travel a different path, we will need to recalibrate how we view our work and the lives we want to lead.

As I was considering business people to interview for the book, I was drawn to the story of Kimberly Samon. Kimberly is a senior human resources executive and corporate attorney. Most recently she was the executive vice president of human resources of a global multibillion-dollar manufacturing company. Her incredible career success and the enormous demands on her time began to clash with the need to spend more quality time with her young daughters and the emerging sense she had that her world was way out of balance. The challenges she has faced, the choices she has made, and the recalibration of her mindset made it obvious to me that her story should be shared in this book.

Kimberly, how would you describe a "meaningful life?"

"I often wondered if the meaning of life and living a meaningful life were really one and the same. To live a meaningful life, one has to ascertain what the meaning of life is and craft his deeds and actions to accomplish this end. I'm not sure I thought about the meaning of life much when I was younger. Of course I always tried to live up to my Christian beliefs but did so without a grand plan in mind. As I've hopefully matured in age and wisdom, I define the meaning of life as doing God's great work on earth, however one defines God. Living a meaningful life then leads me to fulfill that mission through influencing others to achieve their goals and dreams. Whether it is within my family, at work, or in community, I believe a meaningful life requires us to collectively serve one another so that we all become individuals of whom we are proud. Pride builds confidence, and confidence enables people to put themselves before others and serve them, thereby continuing the cycle of creating a meaningful life. While I arrived at my definition some time ago, it took me too long to realize that I was serving the work segment of my life far out of proportion to my family and community. A meaningful life is serving one another (including one's self) in balance."

You struggled with balance and perspective for many years in the various senior roles you held, yet you were able to make needed changes in the last year. What was behind these changes? What was the decision-making process you used to make the choices you eventually made?

"The funny thing is, I felt that I had balance for a long time, or at least I talked myself into believing that I had more balance than I did. When you are enjoying what you do, which for many years I did immensely, it is easy to spend more time on those activities. It wasn't that I didn't enjoy spending time at home with my husband and two girls. I loved it. But we get caught up in all of the things we tell ourselves about the financial stability, good role modeling for the girls, etc. Let's face it, ego also plays a part in the imbalance. For those of us who are motivated by achievement, it is hard to turn it off. The company I was with changed dramatically from a leadership, culture, and values perspective and I found myself not enjoying the people I was working with or believing in the mission of the company. Our former leadership team, of which I was a part, defined what we did not as making widgets but as developing and supporting our people so they could make the best widgets possible. This purpose fit in with how I defined a meaningful life, so it was inspiring to be a part of the team and perpetuate this culture. When the leadership changed and it became about the widget instead of the people, I knew—even though I wouldn't admit it for a long time —that I needed a change. At the same time, my girls were getting older and needed me around more. They say timing is everything, and this was one of those situations where I was spending a lot of time away from my family with people and for a cause I no longer believed in—a very different value proposition than when I loved going to work. My girls needed not just my time but for me to be present when I was home. They needed my patience. They needed my creativity. They needed my seventh-grade math skills. All of this I could not fully give after spending long hours every day in a toxic, unfulfilling environment. I knew it was time to go a few years ago, but I talked myself into staying because of an equity stake I had in the company that was potentially going to monetize in the near future."

Many people would use the word "courageous" to describe your decision to walk away from your successful career as an executive VP of HR at a global manufacturing company. What crossed your mind the day you decided to leave? As you reflect on the decision, how do you feel about it now? Have you been able to carry out the career/life plan you hoped for since your departure?

"Leaving the company was not solely my choice. The CEO and I disagreed on many things. Fortunately, we discussed our disagreements openly, and so when the particular issue arose that led up to my departure, I was not surprised at all by the outcome. If this issue did not come to a head, I would have probably hung on for a transaction. I would have once again convinced myself that the financial stability the money would bring was worth putting off a balanced and meaningful life. Looking back on things now, I really don't even think it was the financial stability that was the draw. My husband and I have been fortunate enough to have made a nice living over the years, and we are not particularly money-focused. For me (and I believe for others who already have a comfortable lifestyle) it was more ego-driven. I can't deny that I liked the sound of making a large sum of money in a financial transaction. Perhaps this is my achievement side taking over again. When I left the company, I retained a portion of my equity which has paid out and the truth is, I don't miss the portion I did not receive. As I have told a former colleague and friend who is no longer with the company and is lamenting the loss of his equity, 'We will make up what we left on the table in more meaningful pursuits and be happier doing it.'

"The day I left, I knew I was leaving a *job* and not a successful career. I knew that I may define that career differently in the future, and I also recognized that I didn't know what that career would look like just then but that I would figure it out. I did not feel anxious at all when I left—I felt relieved on so many levels and guilty on so many others. You see, I had left behind some of the most talented, creative, supportive, and respectful business people with whom I had ever worked. These people were a part of the culture we built under our former leaders. They called me 'the buffer' because I was the last bastion of healthy culture on the senior team. They came to me as a sounding board, for career advice, to get input on new projects, and to help them navigate the dark, rough seas they faced with the new leadership. I felt like I abandoned ship, and it took me some time to come to terms with it. I wondered what it is about most executives (or was it just me?) that cause them to feel guilty about leaving their teams, yet we get up every day and leave our families for hours on end.

"I also knew the day that I left that I would have to work really hard at forcing more balance into my life. I had a contract and was fortunate enough to leave with a severance package, and I really wanted to take some time off. My problem was that I really didn't know how to do that well. I had tried one other time in my career to take time off, and it was very difficult for me to do. I wound up interviewing almost immediately and going back to work less than sixty days later. That was not the plan. This time, I was determined to have a summer vacation with my family, which I had not had in twenty-five years. I have always been good at taking all of my vacation time, but I have not been good at *not* working through my vacation. My husband and I often joked that we never really take vacations, we just have the privilege of working from exotic places. I wanted this summer to be different. I received many phone calls in the weeks after I left my position but told people that I would be beginning a search after the girls returned to school in mid-August. I was able to attend a ballet festival in Canada with my daughter in May without wrapping it around a business trip, which had been the original plan, I was able to make it to all of the end-of-the-school-year events for the girls and then plan a wonderful summer of travel for the entire family."

When did you first recognize your own need to find a different kind of life? What are the various components of a meaningful life from your own experience and from others in your life?

"I think I've long believed in the importance of a meaningful life but didn't really start to pursue a meaningful life until after my first child was born. I had business success at a very young age and am motivated by achievement (and probably back then a fear of failure), so prior to children, my career was almost my sole focus. Toward the end of my first pregnancy and in the middle of a very large acquisition that I was leading on the people integration front, my boss, the CEO, looked me straight in the eye and said, 'Your job now is to be a really good mother.' I thank him every day that he gave me the 'permission' that allowed me to give myself the permission to get some balance, which I did, but not until after I stumbled a bit. He was and still is a great role model. He is a devoted husband, raised four wonderful children, and has had a history of one successful career move after another. I watched him answer his phone in the middle of meetings if it was his wife or children, and I watched him build his reputation with his family as much as he built it with the business community. He would never move from Dallas and passed up career opportunities to keep his family happy. He has a meaningful career and a meaningful life and it has always stuck with me. He taught me that a meaningful life includes being just as good at your 'family' job as your 'work' job, and there are no excuses not to be. I've always tried to mirror this example with my own teams and tell them not to apologize to me or the company for doing the right thing and taking care of their families. I would tell them, 'life happens,' when they would come in to ask for time off, etc. to take care of family matters.

"Two other components of a meaningful life for me are faith and service/charity. I experienced both as part of the great culture that no longer existed at the company I just left. The former CEO was by far the most influential leader for whom I had ever worked. He had faith in God (and never forced his definition of God on anyone) and wasn't afraid to speak of it. Perhaps what was even more powerful in the workplace was his faith in people. He always 'tried to catch people being good' versus being 'bad' and because he believed in people, people never wanted to let him down or disappoint him. He had high expectations of people, and because he treated people with respect and dignity, they did all they could to meet his expectations. Prior to working for this CEO, I had always managed my teams in a similar fashion but sometimes doubted that this style of leadership would work at the executive level. After witnessing how people responded to the CEO and the performance effect it had on the company, I am a true believer.

"Service and charity are very important to me in crafting a meaningful life. I believe that it is our duty to help those less fortunate than us, and not only in the monetary sense. I also believe it is important to serve those around us, particularly those we lead. I've always believed that the job of leadership is to serve those you lead. For some, this is counterintuitive because employees do things for the leader, at the request of the leader, and often for the benefit of the leader. The leader, and in many instances the company, should be serving those who leave their families every day and come to work for the company and the leader. Leaders should serve to provide guidance, training, career advice, encouragement, support, and very honest feedback. It is only through this service that employees will become the best versions of themselves and will in turn learn to serve others. Servant leadership obviously has application outside of the business world.

Along with family, faith, charity, and service, I believe that another important component of a meaningful life is achievement. I've mentioned several times that I am very achievement-oriented. I like to do my best and be recognized for it. Recognition can come in many different forms for me—public praise, quiet satisfaction, monetary rewards, or simply being able to check something off of life's list. I have learned over the years to balance my need for achievement with the other components of what has made life meaningful to me. I have also learned that as I achieved more and more, it gave me the confidence to *have* to achieve less."

What has had the most significant impact on the professional and personal choices you have made?

"As I was building my career, the need for achievement, insecurity, and the fear of failure were all very motivating factors for me. Money also played a role in my younger days. Fortunately, I was able to balance those motivators with my desire for putting others first, being well-respected in my field and always trying to do the right thing. For me, and I think for many of us, the passage of time has a significant impact on our choices in life. We are more mature, usually more financially stable, more confident, and less affected by 'norms' or pre-determined paths in life. I think we also realize that life is short, and when you evaluate where you will spend the time you have left, you make better choices in your forties and fifties than in your twenties and thirties. My husband and I get choked up on our children's birthdays and every first day of school because we realize we are a year closer to them leaving us, which makes us incredibly sad. For three months after I left my most recent position, my eight-year-old asked disbelievingly every day, 'Mommy, are you sure you don't have any meetings today? No phone calls? You'll be home when I get home?' I didn't want ten years to go by, and the then-eighteen-year-old only remembering me never being around because I was working all of the time."

Did you have good role models?

"Yes, I had the good fortune to work for some of the best leaders in business. I witnessed the truly successful ones live meaningful lives through balance and prioritization. They were rewarded with loving families, well-adjusted children, and financial stability. I've also witnessed those leaders who put power and money before all else and have seen broken families and lots of unhappiness. I remember saying to a group of colleagues at my first job after college, 'If we put as much effort into our families as we do into our jobs, the divorce rate would drop by half.'"

Is there a checklist you can offer other professionals to help with the recalibration they need to go through?

"Life is short! Pardon the cliché, but it is true. When I speak to people about the most important things in their lives, they almost always tell me it is family. Yet so many people spend long hours away from their families doing things or working for people they despise. It takes courage to veer off the path that one is on. I think you need to have courage and wisdom before making big changes. At the end of the day, we need to make a living and provide for our families, and the wisdom comes in having a plan.

"Spend a lot of time thinking about what will truly make you happy. Reflect on the nature of the work, the work hours, the work environment, family commitments, the level of lifestyle you will be comfortable living. This is the most important part of the process. Many of us think we don't like our fields when, in fact, we like the work, just not the people for whom we are doing it. I believed that I was tired of corporate America. After much thought, I realized that I loved what I did, I just didn't like the person for whom I was working, which significantly changed my outlook. Remember, people usually quit bosses, not companies, so be sure that you understand the motivation for your desire to change.

"Do research on what types of opportunities are out there. So many times we don't even realize that a particular job or field exists. Browse job sites, bounce ideas off of friends and trusted colleagues, and have an understanding of the landscape before you limit the future possibilities. Also, be aware that what you may love to do as a hobby may not be good as a next job. I *love* to cook, but I could never see myself working late nights in a busy, hot kitchen. Now owning a restaurant... that would be something else!

"Once you have figured out what it is you would like to do, make a financial plan. Will you have to change your lifestyle? Do you need to save some more money? Can you get someone to fund your venture? You want to be sure that you are realistic financially so you can give yourself enough runway to make whatever new venture you have, be it another job or your own company, a success. Naturally, some folks will be more risk averse because of certain financial obligations. I believe there is a big perception out there that people will not be able to replace their incomes in this economy. Talented people will always find well-paying jobs. I have repeatedly heard stories from those who left unhealthy or unbalanced environments, and they have told me that they replaced their incomes and are enjoying life so much more.

"If you are going to a new company, be sure to research it thoroughly so you don't wind up in the same situation you are in now. Speak with former employees, talk to current employees, and pay attention to body language. If you are going to be starting your own venture, build the kind of company for your employees and suppliers that you would want to work for as an employee.

"Have the courage to go for it! I always say to my husband whenever we make any big decision, 'what is the worst that can happen?' This helps us focus on the really important issues and doesn't easily allow us to talk ourselves out of the decision based solely on fear."

Kimberly shared in detail what so many professionals, including myself, have experienced as we shifted our focus from work achievement at any price to a more balanced approach and a life filled with meaning and value. Her mindset shifted over time, while others may experience a more immediate change. Regardless, at some point the path to a meaningful life will lead to a crossroads, and difficult choices will often be required. If we fail to reorient our thinking we are likely to fall into the same harmful routines and never achieve a life filled with more purpose and meaning.

Questions for Reflection

◇ Do I feel as if I am at a crossroads in my life or can I see a time in the future when I will need to make potentially difficult decisions? If so, how will I deal with them?

◇ As I consider the factors that once fueled Kimberly's career (ego, achievement, security, fear of failure, financial success, etc.) am I aware of my own challenges? If so, what are they?

◇ How does Kimberly's checklist resonate with me? Would I add or subtract from it?

◇ One of Kimberly's checklist items is to think about what truly makes her happy. What does my list look like? Am I devoting the majority of my time to pursuing the items on this list?

chapter
FIVE
The Need for Authenticity

*"To be yourself in a world that is constantly
trying to make you something else is
the greatest accomplishment."*
RALPH WALDO EMERSON

Why is it difficult to have the same persona at work and home, among colleagues and with friends? Is authenticity necessary in order to lead a meaningful life? I have observed this problem for years but lately have become more aware of the challenges people have with consistently being "real" and yes, I firmly believe authenticity is a vital part of a meaningful life. In past discussions with friends, I have received blank stares and obvious feelings of discomfort when I advocated for being the same person no matter where we were and transparent about our lives with others. Why is authenticity so uncomfortable?

I suspect the root cause of this occurred for many of us at a young age. The first time we felt pressure to "fit in" with a particular group in school, we began down the path of conformity that only accelerated as we grew older. In college, we may have heard from professors (or parents) that we need to keep work, faith, and our personal lives separate. We may have feared being judged or criticized in those early jobs for sharing anything personal, which only hardens into a compartmentalized mindset as we grow in our careers.

Logic should tell us it is inevitably harmful to suppress our true selves for a sustained period of time, yet many people feel there is no other option. Do you love being a parent but feel awkward about discussing your kids at work? Is expressing your faith important to you, but does perceived intolerance among work colleagues and others keep you from discussing it? Have you ever been faced with a difficult ethical or moral dilemma but remained silent rather than advocate for doing the right thing and risking criticism? I want to believe that deep down most of us desire to be consistently more authentic, but we may not know how to get there.

Obstacles to Authenticity

Let's address some of the obstacles that may prevent us from being authentic. (I am making a base assumption that you agree on some level that authenticity is important and that many of us have a desire to be more open, transparent, and genuine.) I also believe that deep down, most of us want to make a positive impact in the world. Thus—in my opinion—here are a few of the obstacles that inhibit our authenticity:

◇ Lack of self-awareness. Do we even know there's a problem?

◇ Fear of people not liking who we truly are.

◇ Fear of not fitting in.

◇ Fear of being judged.

◇ Fear of persecution for our principles and religious beliefs.

◇ Fear of being passed over for a promotion because we don't fit the corporate mold.

◇ Lack of confidence in our own opinions.

◇ Lack of faith in our convictions.

◇ Lack of courage to defend the truth.

◇ Attachment to an income level and lifestyle that requires unhealthy compromise.

◇ Conforming to society's march toward political correctness, universal tolerance, and acceptance of things that are in direct conflict with our faith, values, and principles.

◇ Relaxing our moral standards because it is easier to go along with the crowd than it is to take a stand.

This list may be as painful for you to acknowledge as it is for me to write, or you may have a different list. The points raised may be unsettling, but confronting them is necessary if we are to pursue and embrace a more authentic life.

Embracing the REAL You

If we stop and reflect on the world in which we live, we will surely see disturbing trends that have been years in the making. Our political system is dysfunctional and our economy is in distress. Families are under constant attack and our children are being bombarded with bad influences. Discussions about God and faith are strongly discouraged in the public square. The line between right and wrong is blurred in the name of an "everything goes" mentality, and speaking up in defense of our values often labels us intolerant.

*"All that is necessary for the triumph of evil is
that good men do nothing."*
EDMUND BURKE

Have you ever replayed pivotal moments of your life in your head and regretted your actions or words? Ever feel a twinge when your mouth said one thing and your heart felt another? Perhaps your conscience is trying to get your attention. Maybe it is time to consistently let our true selves be seen by others (easier said than done, I know). Is there an upside to having the courage to embrace who we really are? The answer is a simple yes. Some of the fruits of authenticity include:

◇ We can achieve a sense of peace when we are not at war with ourselves and live out the values and faith we learned as children in a more transparent way.

◇ Our relationships become deeper and more meaningful when we allow others to see the real us.

◇ We can provide inspiration for others to speak/act up in a way consistent with how they really feel.

◇ We can turn back the cultural tsunami that threatens to swamp us by publicly standing up for our deep-felt convictions and values.

◇ The world can be transformed when the authentic and courageous acts of a few positively influence the actions of many.

We have to challenge the fear that somehow being real is a bad thing. It may be uncomfortable and create some opposition in the short term from individuals not used to it. However, practicing transparency, engaging in honest and open dialogue, and always placing your principles and ethics before advancing your career will bring you greater success in every aspect of your life.

I am sharing these thoughts from my perspective as a father, husband, Catholic, and conservative business person who is very involved in the community. You may have different perspectives and faith backgrounds, but I believe anyone can find value in what I am sharing. Much of the responsibility for what is off track in the workplace, our schools, our communities, and the government is placed on our shoulders—we have been complacent and silent. Our faith, principles, voices, determination, commitment, and votes can make a real and lasting difference in the world if we have the courage to stand up for what we believe. Like the image of a pebble dropped in a calm pond, our individual efforts have a ripple effect and can make an enormous difference in the world.

Beth Valenta, a talent-management and leadership-development professional, is an authentic leader in pursuit of a meaningful life. During our conversation about the book, I was struck by her sincerity, authenticity and the sense of peace she had about her life, faith, family, and career.

Beth, how would you describe a "meaningful life?"

"To me a meaningful life has to incorporate a variety of things. Family—a close and loving family—is critical in my definition of 'meaningful.' This means meals together, family outings, and ongoing conversations. Second, meaningful work. Although we have to work to pay the bills, the work you do should also have meaning. It should be something that you feel is important (for whatever reason) and that you enjoy doing. Community follows work: 'It takes a village.' I believe being part of a community and having close friends you can depend on is important to a meaningful life. The good things in life mean so much more when shared with those who care, and the pains in life are so much easier to bear when shared with others. Finally, belief in God. Although the actual religious practices may vary, I hold that a strong belief in God is important. It provides strength when needed and helps you to focus on the bigger aspects of life."

When did you recognize your own need to pursue a meaningful life? What was the catalyst for you?

"I had a trifecta experience shortly after I graduated from college, which really changed my perspective on life in general. My mother died, I traveled to Israel for the first time, and I moved to a new city. Those three occurrences spurred my interest in my Judaism, which in turn drove a lot of introspection and an involvement in a strong Jewish community. I began a new career which didn't really turn out the way I expected. I had to reexamine what I really liked doing and what I wanted to do with my life."

What has had the most significant impact on the professional and personal choices you have made? What role has your faith played in your decisions?

"My family has had the most significant impact on the choices I have made. In my hierarchy of importance, family is at the top. So whatever choices I make have to support a strong family life. My faith is integrated into every aspect of my family life. Many of the things that we do as a family are based on our religious beliefs. However, these same choices have really supported and driven a close-knit family and community life."

What advice would you offer other professionals who may feel trapped in their jobs who are longing to do more, give more, and achieve more in life?

"We all have to do what we have to do to support ourselves and our family. Sometimes (especially in these challenging economic times) that means working at a job that isn't ideal. While you might not be able to change that, you certainly aren't helpless. There are things individuals can do to better position themselves for positive career change and to make their current situation more meaningful."

Beth, I am interested in your reference to working at a job that is not "ideal." How can professionals be successful in that kind of environment?

"In terms of careers, networking and getting involved in professional organizations can help position you to move to a better work situation as the economy improves. Talking with people who value your input or who may be in similar situations can also help you feel better about yourself and your current situation.

"While you might not be able to change your work situation in the short-term, I believe you can add value by giving back to others. This can include mentoring and paying it forward with job help to others. Or it might be achieved by doing volunteer work in some area that has meaning to you. If you can incorporate some of the things that are important to you through those avenues, it will make the wait to get your career on track a little easier."

Beth, do you believe that pursuing a life filled with meaning and purpose is achievable for everyone? If so, what are the obstacles holding so many people back?

"I do believe that a life of meaning is available to everyone. That definition of meaning will vary by person, of course. I think the things that hold people back are fear and inertia. Fear of making a change, fear of the unknown, fear of letting down their family. Inertia says an object at rest stays at rest. It's hard to make a change. It requires a lot of time and effort. Not everyone is willing or able to muster the energy to push forward to make the changes needed."

How would you describe this stage of your life?

"I am truly blessed. I have a wonderful and loving family, a great and supportive set of friends and community, and a strong belief in God. The one area I still struggle with is finding the right path to long-term career satisfaction. However, I have a plan which I'm executing against, and I choose to focus on the positive aspects of where I am now."

Another person with great insight into the topic of authenticity and the meaningful life is Richard Smith. Richard is a seasoned consulting professional with more that twenty years of experience and success in cultural transformation, talent management, corporate diversity, and talent acquisition. He started his career with the nonprofit organization Inroads, and then he held a variety of corporate and consulting roles before launching his own consulting firm, Benton Bradford.

Richard, what role does authenticity play as you consider the subject of this book?

"My life has meaning when I am able to contribute to the lives of others while at work. This can take the form of consultation on work-related items or advice to someone on how to advance his or her career. It's when I am able to contribute to someone in a way that is meaningful and impactful.

"It also means being able to have a wonderful life and relationship with my wife and my family. It's those relationships that give me the support and nourishment that I need in order to deal with the demands of my working life. Spending time with my wife and family recharges me and helps me to continue to do the work I enjoy outside of the home.

"Having meaning in my life means that I am living my best authentic life in accordance to key values and principles that allow me to fully be who I am and can be."

You have been very intentional about the path in your career, starting with a nonprofit, gaining corporate experience, and now building your own consulting business. When did you know where you were headed? What was the motivation for these decisions in your life?

"I didn't know where I was headed until the beginning of 2012 after I was laid off from my last role and I did an assessment of the kind of life I wanted and the work I wanted to do within companies. It became clear to me that I could make a living and make my consulting business work when I let go of fear and followed my passion. I was recently offered a full-time role with one of my clients and turned it down because it meant that I have to make concessions that would have gone against my values. There would have been a time when I would have made that concession, but now it's not possible. I didn't want to be chained to my paycheck and to a job that would have compromised who I really am and what I value in life.

"I also held myself back because I was letting the fear of never getting another project paralyze me. I certainly have concerns from time to time. However, I am able to manage through that fear with a plan and hard work."

What is important to you now versus twenty years ago?

"Before it was the quantity of things that I did that was important to me. The more I did the better it felt to me. But now I focus on the quality of my life, being real, and my relationships. I have established core principles about how I want to live my life, and I do my best to follow them every day. These core principles are faith, passion, and purpose. Faith in Allah and that path that he has for me; passion about my life and my relationships; and fulfilling my core purpose to add value to those I come in contact with each and every day."

One of the threads running through my conversations with Beth and Richard is their abundance of emotional maturity formed by their years of experience and the people in their lives. Being "authentic" requires a mature self-awareness that is not easily granted to the young and inexperienced but is something to be savored and appreciated when it is attained.

After you read this chapter and reflect on Beth and Richard's interviews, please consider if you are being authentic to those around you. Let's set a good example for others by being unafraid to be our true selves and stand up for our beliefs. What is required of us is not easy but necessary if we want change. Our acts of courage and authenticity, no matter how small, can join together with others to make a positive difference in the world and inspire others to pursue more meaningful lives.

Questions for Reflection

◇ Do I feel comfortable sharing who I really am and what I truly think with my co-workers? Am I self-aware enough to know if I am being authentic or not? If not, why not?

◇ How does the topic of authenticity in this chapter connect with the concept of the integrated life in the last chapter?

◇ Am I challenged by any of the obstacles to authenticity that Randy Hain shared at the beginning of the chapter? How will I overcome these?

◇ Beth and Richard's lives seem to be in balance with their priorities in order, and they are transparent about their beliefs and expectations. Do I emulate Beth and Richard in this regard? Why or why not (and how could I)?

chapter
SIX
Leading an Integrated Life

"It was clear that my former method of leading
a compartmentalized life would
no longer suffice."

hy focus on integration? After college until I turned forty, I struggled with integration as I kept the different areas of my life rigidly compartmentalized. I have recognized this challenge in many of the professionals I have encountered over the years. Why is this such an issue? I believe for many of us we are trained at an early age to lead separate lives, and this is typically encouraged in the workplace. This is certainly the case for those who are especially fearful of integrating their faith with their work. I dealt with this subject more deeply in the previous chapter on authenticity, but here we will address the overall issue of integrating all aspects of our lives together and of being consistent about who we are and what we want in life. Prior to my conversion to the Catholic Church in 2005, I had lived more than twenty years in what I call the "spiritual wilderness," a period when I had no faith in my life. I kept my work life and family life very separate and often, I am ashamed to say, my family existed for my work instead of the other way around. My conversion experience changed everything for me, and the seeds of my passion for integration were firmly planted.

With my new priorities established as faith first, family second, and work third, how could I live my life in a way which would be pleasing to God? It was clear that my former method of leading a compartmentalized life would no longer suffice. I needed to lead an integrated life where I could be the same person all the time and put his will first in every aspect of my life. You may not feel that leading an integrated life is important or that faith is not a key component, but consider how damaging it is to lead separate lives with one for work, one for home, and one for your place of worship. Even if you have little or no faith in your life, I hope you will acknowledge how fundamentally unhealthy it is to lead divided lives. I challenge all of us to lead one life with consistency and authenticity (which is a theme we explored in the previous chapter).

One person who has long held my respect for a number of reasons, especially the way she leads an integrated life, is Tami Heim. Tami is a former senior executive with Federated Department Stores, president of Border's Book Stores, EVP and chief publishing officer for Thomas Nelson Publishing, and is currently the CEO of the Christian Leadership Alliance. Tami has long lived her professional life with her faith at the heart of everything she does and enjoys a stellar reputation for her business acumen, leadership, and strong values around the country. I recently caught up with the Nashville, Tennessee, resident to discuss her views on leading a meaningful life.

Tami, I am thrilled to gather your thoughts on how integration helps you lead a meaningful life. What does a "meaningful life" look like to you?

"A meaningful life is one where I have the freedom to walk in confidence and humility every day in every way because I know who I am and whose I am in Christ. This revelation of who I am, who he is, and how my life fits into his plan gives me perspective, orders my priorities, and gives meaning to everything I do."

To many, a meaningful life is primarily all about finding work/life balance. You obviously see it as much more than simply balance. What are the various components of a meaningful life from your own experience and from others in your life?

"It seems like this is a critical need that people express wherever I go. For many it is a vain quest. In fact, I will go so far to say I find the concept of balance or the urgent need for it to be grossly distorted. It implies that there is an equalness in all areas of life to be achieved. The shadows of a world view are cast all over it. Nowhere in Scripture are we called to have life-balance. Actually Scripture gives us clear direction on how to live our life, and there is no evenness about it. Scripture clearly reveals God's expectations and priorities for living a meaningful life:

> 'You shall love the Lord your God with all your heart, and with all your soul, and with all your mind.' This is the greatest and first commandment. And a second is like it: 'You shall love your neighbour as yourself.' On these two commandments hang all the law and the prophets.
>
> MATTHEW 22:37–40

"When I look at the way I spend my days and interact with others, I challenge myself with this Scripture. I want this outcome to influence all I do. When I am resolved to be faithful with these two commands, my days are humbling and deeply gratifying.

"There is a sweet and holy integration in life when I follow what God directs. To give my whole mind, heart, and soul to something pretty much means I am saturated to the point where my daily life becomes an overflow of my devotion. Life is congruent with God's attitude and his priorities. But getting to this place of godly balance requires time and devotion.

"It is only as I commit myself to the disciplines of reading the Bible, praying, waiting, and listening to God's direction that I get closer to his plan and priorities for my life. It's there that life has its most absolute meaning. One thing I know for sure, when I get my God-balance on, there is nothing more glorious or rewarding."

Faith has long been central to your life. Did this "launch" your desire for a different kind of life?

"It all came together for me in a profound way on the day after I graduated from college. I surrendered the control of my life to Christ and in that moment God rewrote the text of my life and replaced my ambition for his. My after-college 'plan' was abandoned for his. I immediately began to trust and obey what his Word said was true, and my life started to work out in ways I never imagined possible."

How do you make decisions at this point in your life? Is there a difference between now and the beginning of your career?

"I've never made a big decision, personally or professionally, that was not bathed in prayer and confirmation. As I get older I find myself praying over everything—my day, schedule, conversations, projects, what to do next, and how to listen to others so that I hear their true hearts. I'm always asking for wisdom and discernment. I never want a day to pass where I miss standing and observing the *awe* of God in and around me."

Is there guidance you can offer the readers of this book on the way to pursue and lead an integrated and meaningful life?

"Certainly! This is advice I have given often throughout my life:

— "Choose your attitude every day. Choose how you feel about where you are in your career, with your family, and your life. You are only a victim or trapped by your circumstances because you choose it.

— "Accept. Wholeheartedly accept that where you are right now is exactly where God wants you to be.

— "Be grateful. Gratitude changes your perspective on everything.

— "Rejoice. Rejoice—with everything within you—in all situations and lovingly yield yourself to whatever God wants to do in and through you.

— "Pay attention, be present, and be all in. Faithfulness in responding to what God has for you right now, in the moment you are in, will always point you to what he has next for you.

"I've experienced nine significant transitions in my life. I was once asked to share my thoughts on transitions for a Women in Leadership group. They were interested in how I knew a transition was at hand. I took the time to prayerfully review each of them again and discovered there were several things consistently true:

— "I'd given the best of me.

— "I finished strong.

— "It was easy for me to move on and for someone else to move in.

— "Mutual love and respect were present among those I left.

— "While the people who filled my day-to-day life changed, our relationships remained intact.

— "Every change provided me an opportunity to engage deeper with my family and those closest to me.

— "On the other side of every transition, God had a desire of my heart waiting for me; the kind of desires so deep within me I never had the courage to hear my voice utter them.

"And while these events signaled transition and a time of change, there were several things that never changed:

— "God's love for me.

— "My love for God.

— "There was always more than one new door open to consider.

— "The next assignment was never anything I ever imagined.

— "My next position was completely outside of my comfort zone

— "My desperate need for his wisdom and strength was greater in that moment than it had ever been in the past."

Since 2005, much of my writing and ministry work in the Catholic Church has been in the area of fostering the idea of leading a fully integrated life. My efforts around daily prayer, stewardship, servant leadership, and becoming a better leader, husband, and father have been blessed because I now have strong faith and that is what binds it all together. The intent in sharing my perspective on the integrated life and Tami Heim's interview is to show ways we can alter our lives in a way that assimilates faith, family, and work and puts us on the path to a life filled with meaning. I try every day to do the actions I have shared, and I assure you that I struggle like anyone else. The challenge is to practice them not as a bunch of new "to-dos" but as part of a broader, unifying approach to a balanced and meaningful life.

I believe we are faced with a choice between a compartmentalized life or an integrated life where faith, family, and work are unified and centered in our relationship with our Creator. My hope is that everyone undergoes a true metamorphosis and leads an integrated, balanced and meaningful life. It isn't easy, but it is worth the journey, and I know those who have been successful have seen their lives transformed for the better. I encourage you to begin tomorrow with a firm disposition to be more aware of the self-created walls in your life and begin the process of tearing them down. It will take self-awareness, prayer, candid input from trusted friends, and courage, but the result will be worth it!

Questions for Reflection

◇ Do I ever feel like I am two or even three distinctly different people during the day based on my environment and companions?

◇ What value do I see in leading an integrated life and changing the compartmentalized way I have been living? Why?

◇ Have I ever considered the role faith plays in my work, community-service, and family life? What are ways I can bring my "faith personality" into the other areas of my life?

◇ What can I learn from Tami's example and the way she lives out her life?

chapter
SEVEN
Leveraging Our Gifts and Achieving Greatness

"People who are making a difference are doing so by honing their gifts every day. It becomes like a well-defined muscle. To keep the muscle strong, you have to use your gifts frequently."

One aspect of leading a meaningful life I most enjoy observing is when people leverage their talents and gifts in the service of others. On occasion, some of these gifted individuals achieve a level of greatness. This is greatness not defined by power and wealth but by the way they live their lives, serve God, and give back to the world. Two individuals who have always had my admiration and respect for how they use their gifts are Glen Jackson and Dr. Paul Voss. In my opinion and the opinion of countless others, these men have both attained greatness in their own ways, but both are too humble to ever be comfortable with this label. I have long looked forward to interviewing them for this book.

Glen Jackson is a husband, father, faithful Christian, community servant, and successful business leader. He is the president and co-founder of Jackson Spalding, a full-service image-creation, cultivation, and communications firm with a stellar national reputation. Glen is one of the kindest men you will ever meet and is insatiably curious about other people. His work in the nonprofit community has helped him leave a legacy of work well-done, and he is an example for other servant leaders to emulate. I caught up with Glen in the summer of 2012 to discuss the topic of this book and had a chance to ask him several questions:

Glen, I am grateful for a chance to chat with you about my new book and share views on the meaningful life! Let's start there. How do you define a meaningful life?

"A life of meaning is all about serving others. It is not about self. Whether you have a meaningful life or not is best defined by those who know you best, starting with your family. It is the people whom you have loved, influenced, served, uplifted, offered grace to, and touched with your heart who verify your meaningfulness.

"I also believe a life of real substance is not about money or power or accumulating material things. It requires patience, perseverance, humility, generosity, and possessing a genuine relationship with God. If you have a meaningful life, one thing is guaranteed: You will have a powerful legacy, one that impacts multiple generations, multiple age groups, and diverse backgrounds."

Glen, how do challenges of everyday life fit into this?

"I believe you can't have a meaningful life without pain and sorrow. The most meaningful people I know have withstood some terrible tragedy or tragedies, refusing to give up as they are refined like silver. It is their enduring and perhaps conquering of an obstacle that makes their life more profound and richer and ennobling. When you have rich stories to tell about your life, it can serve as a spur for those people who hear your stories; they, in turn, are encouraged in their own journey to make a difference and live a life that demands an explanation. A life that is about character success, not circumstance success. A life that pierces the veneer of outside things."

What role do a person's gifts play in your definition of a meaningful life?

"People who are leading a life that demands an explanation—a meaningful life—all have something in common: They love to leverage their gifts. To do this effectively, they first know what their gifts are. We all have different talents, and I believe all us of have more than one. If you are unsure what your gifts are, ask a trusted friend. He or she will tell you. People who are making a difference are doing so by honing their gifts every day. It becomes like a well-defined muscle. To keep the muscle strong, you have to use your gifts frequently. One of my gifts is encouraging people. To keep this muscle at peak performance, I try to encourage someone every day with an uplifting word or a gesture, such as a smile or a handwritten note or even a text. One of my favorite things to do is pull up a contact on my phone while driving to or from work and give this person a call just to say hello. The wonderful gift here is when you refresh others you actually refresh yourself.

"Too many people associate gifts with money. Look beyond the mighty dollar and open your eyes to gifts that are inside of you—such as encouragement, prayer, discernment, leadership, and mercy. These gifts can have an eternal difference, especially giving someone your time and serving as a listening ear."

I know you to be a man of strong faith. How has your faith shaped you and helped you on your personal and professional journey?

"One of the 'must haves' in the meaningful-life formula is faith. God wants to be our biggest encourager and help us to do meaningful things. Sadly, too few people give him the opportunity to help make the meaningful happen. He is the maestro. Give him the baton.

"I like the Dutch proverb that says, 'Who we are is God's gift to us. What we become is our gift to him.' It is hard to be thankful in all circumstances, but that is where God—through his Son and our Savior Jesus—wants us to be. To rejoice always. To pray constantly.

To be thankful in all things. I try to use this formula a lot in my life. It keeps my chin up and reminds me to strive every day to be a person of impact. Now you can't be a person of impact if you have self-doubt or lack a clear conscience. These impediments can be formidable, a real albatross around your neck. My quiet time in the morning, essential time, helps me deal with these types of issues. I have a special place in my home where I go to be quiet and listen to God. Without this time, I am a 'sitting duck' for life's trials and tribulations. As a result, I can't be a Psalm 112 person.

"Psalm 112 is a matchless Psalm in that it shows us specifically what a meaningful life looks like. Try reading Psalm 112 for thirty days and see what happens. I hope and pray that it will inspire you to raise the bar in terms of how your life can impact others."

Glen, you have an inspirational story and one many want to emulate. Do you think the meaningful lives you and others in this book are leading are attainable?

"Yes. Now I know there are people in the workplace who might feel trapped. They want to do more and achieve more. To them I say, if you feel this way, start praying about it. Ask God where he wants to use you. Ask him to get you outside your comfort zone. Ask for courage and wisdom.

"Sarah Young's book *Jesus Calling* is a terrific devotional to read in the morning to help you hear God's whispers. The book is anointed. Seek answers to your questions about feeling trapped with a humble heart. Reach out to friends you trust because of their wisdom. Be open and candid with them. Ask for their help and prayers. Soon what once was foggy will become clear. Don't be surprised if God, through the Bible and circumstances, poses to you a lot of questions. That is OK. The Book of Job has more than 200 questions, most asked by God to Job.

"I like the story, it is taped on my desk, about the man who stood at the 'gate of the year' and asked for a light so he may tread safely into the unknown. He heard this response in return: 'Go out into the darkness and put your hand into the hand of God. That shall be to you better than light and safer than a known way.' Safer than a known way is what faith means to me. In my life, I have seen the value of trusting that hand when everything around you feels dark."

It is interesting that we were talking about using our natural God-given gifts, but now we are talking about other gifts from God. Right?

"Right. The Bible is one such gift, and it is a balm that helps me deal with my fears. If you were to look at any life of meaning, you will see that this person is fearless but never hopeless. Fear can be so paralyzing. Perfection is paralysis, especially for men. I try to make sure in my life that I focus more on progress than perfection. We all slip and fall. If we didn't, we would not need a savior to pick us up. It is when I fall that I feel closest to God as I witness firsthand his unconditional love for me. Corrie ten Boom, who wrote *The Hiding Place*, one of my favorite books, a book about courage and faith in World War II, said this once about dealing with the unknown:

— "'When you are on a train and it goes through a tunnel and the world suddenly goes dark, do you jump out? Of course not. You sit still and trust. You trust the engineer to get you through the tunnel. Trust is another of God's gifts. Keep trusting, especially when in any kind of life tunnel, sickness, depression, joblessness, a prodigal child, etc. and your life will be meaningful beyond words. Your life will be a gift to others and, most of all, to God. Strength for the journey!'"

I find Glen's inspirational outlook on the world and candid assessment of the meaningful life to be an important contribution to this book. At the root of it all is the bedrock of his Christian faith and his belief that he is called to serve others through the gifts he has been given. Dr. Paul Voss is a loving husband and father, devoted Catholic, sought-after speaker, college professor, and the president and co-founder of Ethikos and Areté Leadership Group. Ethikos is a national consulting firm that provides consulting and coaching for the Fortune 1000 in the areas of ethics and transformational leadership. Areté Leadership Group is a leading executive training and leadership membership organization dedicated to helping busy executives and managers "see the bigger picture" in their professional and personal development.

I have known Dr. Voss for years and have long respected his dedication to faith and family as well as the significant impact he has made on business professionals (and their thinking) around the country through his talks and writing. In our interview, he takes the idea of leveraging gifts a little further and explores the idea of "greatness":

Dr. Voss, we have spoken many times about pursuing lives filled with meaning. I would like to dive into an aspect of the meaningful life you have mentioned to me before: the concept of greatness. How do people achieve greatness?

"'Some are born great; some achieve greatness; and some have greatness thrust upon them.' This quote, written by William Shakespeare, captures (I think) a reality we see operating in our lives and the world around us. It does indeed seem that the 'natural lottery of talent' favors some over others. Not everyone can be an Olympic champion or a Nobel Prize-winning physicist, and we all know people of extraordinary talent who seem especially 'blessed.' Some people were born with superb genes and God-given talents. We often say that such people 'were born to play the violin' or 'born to design a building.'

"Other successful people combine native ability and conspicuous hard work—often from sheer force of the will—to achieve extraordinary success in business, athletics, and academics. We respect and admire these folks because they represent the American dream of the 'self-made man' by employing self-reliance and pulling themselves up from their own bootstraps to create great careers."

What about those who don't possess the same natural talents or those who face great adversity. How do they attain greatness? Is there a difference between greatness and excellence?

"Well, some 'have greatness thrust upon them' as they rise to a situation when confronting a job loss, death in the family, or horrific event. These folks experience a baptism by fire and can achieve greatness—as when the backup quarterback replaces the injured starter and rallies the team to victory. We often say that this player 'had a great game.'

"But greatness differs from 'excellence' in important ways. Greatness often describes a moment in time—a single event or a period of time in one career. Excellence covers a lifetime and refers to behavior, deportment, integrity, character, and conduct. In other words, one can be great (in politics, business, or athletics) without being excellent. Moreover, no one is born excellent. One cannot have excellence thrust upon them. Excellence, to borrow from Aristotle, requires virtuous action habitually repeated. The virtues highlighted by Aristotle as the cardinal virtues (from the Latin word for 'hinge' or 'pivot') have resonance for both personal and professional life. These virtues—prudence, justice, temperance, and fortitude—are the building blocks of excellence for any person, family, team, firm, company, or organization."

Do you have gifts? Are you using them? To what end? Do you aspire to achieve greatness? Would not excellence be a more appropriate pursuit on the path to a meaningful life? These are the questions raised by the insightful conversations I had with Glen Jackson and Dr. Paul Voss. Consider your own life. Have you achieved greatness in any area of your life? Did you know that it is also "great" to be an excellent parent, loving spouse, selfless leader, good steward, faithful friend, dedicated employee, and to be blessed with strong faith? I make this distinction because having gifts and achieving greatness or excellence can sometimes create images in our minds of often unattainable goals. Take an inventory of your gifts and if you are not sure, ask someone you trust. Once you have reviewed the list, make a parallel list of where you have applied those gifts in helping others. What did you learn from this exercise? This can be a most instructive (and humbling) way of evaluating the use of gifts in pursuing more meaningful lives.

Please consider that an important aspect of living a meaningful life can often mean we use our modest gifts to help others in small ways, never achieving prominence but making a difference nonetheless. Headlines and glory should not matter, and we may achieve greatness only in the eyes of our loved ones because of the sacrifices we make to provide for our families.

Questions for Reflection

◇ How am I using my gifts to make a difference in the lives of others? Have I thought of this as important before now?

◇ Glen Jackson said leading a meaningful life means leaving a legacy. What kind of legacy will I leave behind for family, friends, and the world? Am I leaving a legacy or looking for glory?

◇ Is it difficult for me to be outward-focused versus inward-focused? Do I think of others before myself? If not, how can I change?

◇ Dr. Voss shared helpful insight into the concept of greatness. In my own way, how have I achieved "greatness" in the last few years? Am I working toward excellence?

chapter
EIGHT
The Illusion of Success

*"As you pursue a meaningful life, how will you
know if you have been successful and if
your current definition of success is
holding you back?"*

M y father came to our house for a visit last summer, which he typically does two or three times a year. He loves to see his grandsons, and we talk to him every week by phone, but it is sometimes difficult for him to travel from his Florida home to Atlanta. I have occasionally written about my dad over the years and the wise counsel and good example I have always received from him. This particular weekend visit was different because of a powerful lesson he helped me teach my eleven-year-old son.

On the Saturday afternoon of my dad's visit, my younger son and I were throwing the baseball outside while my father was taking a short nap in his room. I can always tell when one of my boys has something on his mind, so I probed and asked him if everything was all right. He responded with, "Dad, remember when we talked about what it means to be successful a few weeks ago? Is Papa successful?"

Wow! That was an interesting and mature question from my younger child. He was referring to a conversation we had a few months ago about being successful in business and what kind of career he wanted to have after college. I gave him a thoroughly modern version of what I thought success looked like in business and made sure we talked about having strong faith and the importance of starting and caring for a family some day as well. I kept it at a high level for him at that time, but his question about my father deserved a deeper answer.

I explained that my father came from a different generation. He was in the Army for six years after high school and then he completed two years of college before going to work full time. He met and married my mother, who also worked for his company in 1965, and I came along in 1966. We didn't have a lot of extras when I was growing up, but we had what we needed. Both my parents worked, but we always had dinner together, and my father frequently coached my sports teams. They were both active volunteers at church. Even though my parents did not finish college, they both instilled in me a passion for learning when I was young, and there was no question in their minds that I would be continuing my education after high school. The same was true for my younger sister.

Our father and mother taught us about faith and the value of hard work. We knew how to be self-sufficient at a young age. Strong values and great life lessons were instilled in us from my earliest childhood memories. So is my father successful? By modern standards, a quick glance at his meager savings and lack of material possessions would merit a resounding "no." But in the areas that mattered most to him and also to my mother while she was alive, they were incredibly blessed all their lives with everything they could ever desire.

You see, my parents never tried to keep up with the Joneses. Acquiring toys and wealth never mattered. They were focused on raising us as faith-filled children, helping as much as possible with furthering our education and teaching us how to be responsible. When I call him today, my father always wants to talk about the kids' school and athletic achievements or find out how my books are selling. He rarely talks about himself, and he certainly never complains.

He comes from a generation that has much to teach us. We can deceive ourselves all we want that today's world holds us to a different standard, but as I get older I recognize that we also have the ability to choose the lives we want to lead. The more I detach myself from modern society's view of success, the happier and more fulfilled I feel. This detachment allows me to put the appropriate focus on serving God and my faith, raising my children, loving my wife, and giving back to others instead of accumulating toys that become false idols. I learned these invaluable lessons from my parents—especially my father.

So, back to that question from my young child: Is Papa successful? I told my son, "You know, I think my father is the most successful man I know. I hope I am half the man he is when I am his age." "Thanks Dad," my son said. "I think you and Mom are doing a pretty good job." In light of the last chapter on gifts and greatness, this is probably the most validating statement I could ever want!

The idea of success that many of us are taught at a young age is often an illusion that can create frustration, anxiety, and years of wasted time as we wind up chasing something that may not be what we need or want as we continue to grow older. My father was wise enough to avoid this trap and has done his best to convey the lesson to me, although I must admit I spent several years in the quicksand of pursuing false success. In order to shed more light on the idea of success, I reached out to a Boston-based business leader and author I have gotten to know over the last year who has a fascinating story and candid thoughts on what success really means. His name is Andreas Widmer.

Andreas is director of Entrepreneurship Programs at The Catholic University of America and president of The Carpenter's Fund, a startup that seeks to provide loans to emerging-market small- and medium-sized enterprises. He was previously the co-founder of SEVEN Fund, a philanthropic organization which promoted enterprise solutions to poverty. He is also the author of *The Pope & The CEO: Pope John Paul II's Lessons to a Young Swiss Guard*, a book exploring leadership lessons that he learned serving as a Swiss Guard protecting Pope John Paul II and refined during his career as a successful business executive.

Andreas, thank you for taking time for this conversation. Considering the fascinating life you lead, I am curious how you would describe a "meaningful life."

"Becoming fully human—that is to say, one's intellectual, physical, social, emotional, and spiritual fulfillment which, with God's grace, will lead to eternal life with God."

What are the various aspects of a meaningful life from your own experience and from others in your life? Does balance play a part?

"The point of 'balance' is to become fully human. People with a meaningful life live it as authentically human persons. Part of that is that we're not meant to be lopsided toward one of the aspects of our humanity because that makes us less human. Another part of it that we often overlook is the true aspect of the social life, where it is in giving that we receive. The pursuit of the meaningful life as a human person cannot be fed by an egotistical self-centeredness. It has to be nurtured by sacrificial love or it won't be truly human—truly in the image and likeness of God."

You have shared with me that you are not the same man and leader you once were. What did you mean?

"I lived for over ten years in the myopic pursuit of economic success. I gained it. Then I lost it. The experience made me realize that having the money (and not having it) actually didn't provide meaning or happiness, so I set out to find meaning elsewhere."

Did your Catholic faith play a significant role in the professional and personal choices you have made? Did it help you recognize that the success you were striving for was an illusion?

"It does now. Through the influence of my faith I live my life much more consciously. It sounds contradictory, but my faith helps me focus more on the moment and on eternity at the same time. It's one of those beautiful 'both-and' things of our faith."

What advice would you offer other professionals who are longing to do more, give more, and achieve more in life?

"Find time to pray, read the Bible and religious books. Develop a habit to journal your intuitions and the events around you. I find a good balance to be to pray both in contemplation and in conversation. In the former, I love the rosary and/or an adoration. For the latter, I like journaling and then having a discussion with God. You'd be surprised how much change comes from it. The key is that you trust God. Once you are led in a certain direction, work as hard on it as you can, but trust God that he'll take care of things."

Andreas, what prevents so many people from pursuing this kind of life?

"If you want to attain any level of happiness in your life, you better pursue a life of meaning and purpose. What's holding us back is a fear of letting go of our self-centeredness."

How do you balance your professional life, teaching, writing, and philanthropy? How would you describe this stage of your life?

"My first priority is my relationship with God. My second priority is my relationship with my wife and my son. My third priority is my professional career. It's in that order that I try to evaluate decisions. Often they're intertwined, but I always know what the right decision is if I'm honest with myself.

"Also, my wife and I have an ongoing written 'plan' for our life. We meet every year to review last year's 'plan' and create the new year's plan. In it we describe what's important to us and what we'll do about it this year. We discuss this a few times during the year as well to check where we're at. It's been incredible how this has focused our actions and helped us achieve things.

"My current stage in life? I'm at the point where I've started to know how little I know. So that breeds humility and gratefulness. It also helps me be less afraid of the future because it allows me to trust God much more. That's made a great difference in my life and happiness.

Think about how you grew up and your first few years in the workforce. It is likely you were trained to achieve success through climbing the corporate ladder and making a good living. These things in themselves are not bad, but they become negative if we define ourselves and who we really are by mere economic success and titles. The stories of my father and Andreas Widmer remind us of the importance of trusting God's role in our lives, the need for humility, gratitude, and to be focused on serving others. I also think it is a subtle yet important point to recognize that both men receive their validation not through awards and the trappings of material success, but through their success as parents, husbands, and servants of God and to their communities. Andreas had it all, lost it and has since attained a new and authentic degree of success as he puts his gifts to use in serving God and his fellow man. My father has spent most of his life disinterested in anything other than becoming the best husband, father, grandfather, and selfless servant he can be. He has never missed the illusion of success that drives so many others. Andreas experienced his own crucible of painful lessons to emerge in much the same place.

Consider what it is you are currently chasing in your life and ask yourself if you are fulfilled. As you consider the pursuit of a meaningful life, how will you know if you have been successful, and is your current definition of success truly making you happy?

Questions for Reflection

◇ What does success mean to me now versus ten years ago? Twenty? How do I define it?

◇ Have I considered the role of humility and service to others in considering success?

◇ How do I receive personal validation today? Is it encouragement from my loved ones? My name on a plaque? What?

◇ As I reflect on my views about success, do I need to rethink and change how I might teach these lessons to my children and grandchildren?

chapter NINE

Should I Stay or Should I Go?

*"Some of the issues these professionals were hoping to escape
also exist in their new organization...because the problem
or issue frequently lies within themselves. This misguided move can often derail the pursuit
of a richer and fuller life."*

One of the crucial components of achieving a meaningful life is your job, and you should carefully evaluate if you can attain this goal where you are or if you need to pursue a new career elsewhere, as leaving for the wrong reasons can be a big mistake. Have you recently received a call from a recruiter about a new opportunity that got you thinking? Perhaps you're feeling underappreciated by your boss. Are there too few opportunities for professional growth at your company? Are you experiencing financial challenges? Have the leaders failed to inspire you because of a lack of vision? Maybe you're just bored. All seemingly acceptable reasons to start polishing that résumé...or are they?

From hundreds of professional friends and acquaintances over the years, I have heard these and many other motives as why people want to leave a job. While advising all kinds of potential job seekers, I recently began pondering the question, "When is it time to *not* leave a job?"

It is a legitimate question that generally receives little thought or reflection. We are often quick to find an escape route, but we don't spend enough time trying to improve our situation or change our mindset. Is this necessary? Absolutely. The reality is that people who change jobs often don't find the proverbial greener pastures with a new company. Some of the issues these professionals were hoping to escape also exist in their new organization...because the problem or issue frequently lies within themselves. This misguided move can often derail the pursuit of a richer and fuller life filled with meaning.

Karen Steadman, a principal with Leadership Futures, shares this insight: "People sometimes mistakenly believe their strengths will be better understood by a new group of people and that their weaknesses will no longer stand out. However, the best predictor of future performance is past performance unless significant changes or learning have taken place. It may be unrealistic to think that the next organization is a magical, perfect fit if nothing else about the person has changed in the interim."

After a little self-reflection, would-be job seekers tend to realize they own many of the issues they have in their careers. So perhaps leaving a job is not always the most advantageous route to take. Turn the eyes inward first. Why do people work? The majority of us would likely say to support ourselves or our families. Many would say we work because we like our chosen field and find it intellectually stimulating. Others enjoy the challenge their jobs offer and feel they are making a positive difference. And there are those who enjoy the relationships they have formed.

Finding a job and a company that provides all of the above is a tall order. Sometimes we expect too much, and when we don't get it, frustration is a likely result. Is it naïve to think our jobs will bring total happiness? Among candidates ranging from recent college graduates to senior executives in transition to employed potential job seekers, a central theme runs through most conversations: They have the desire to "have it all" in their career. They want that next role to have a check next to all the boxes on the ideal job list. There are certainly exceptions, but generally speaking, very few jobs are able to meet these expectations. So where does that leave us?

Leaving an existing job for another is not a step to be taken lightly. There is much to be considered and investigated before such a move is made. Make time for practical thinking and consider this checklist before making a change:

Do a skills inventory. Where do your strengths lie? What do you have to offer that is unique? Is your current job mining these skills or are you feeling underused?

Do a needs inventory. What specific needs do you have that are not being met? Is it intellectual stimulation? Mentoring? More challenge? Higher income? Loftier title? More balance? Flexible hours? Whatever is on your list needs to be realistic (a new convertible BMW company car is unlikely!) and something you have the courage to discuss with your manager.

Identify repairs needed. What are your development areas? Be honest about what you need to work on professionally and personally and consider if you are getting this assistance in your current role. Please realize that your manager is not clairvoyant, so be forthcoming about what you need if you ever hope to receive it.

Are you aligned? Does your job utilize your education and training? Does your compensation align with your experience and market value (check out salary.com)? Are you on an appropriate and realistic career trajectory?

What are the expectations? A common mistake with people frustrated at work is the failure to clarify what is expected of them, says Brandon Smith, founder of theworkplacetherapist.com. Most would rather guess, usually guess wrong, and end up in frustration, according to Smith. Additionally, it is important to know what is expected of your boss, as this is helpful in making your own expectations clear.

What are you passionate about? This is important. I think most of us want to feel that what we are doing is worthwhile and making a positive difference. Make a list of what is important to you and determine if your current job will allow you to pursue your noble, overarching goals.

Are your values in sync with your job? This is an area we should never have to compromise, but too often people conceal their true selves and personal values for the sake of their career. Ask yourself if you are free to be your authentic self at work or if you feel compelled to make unhealthy compromises in order to fit in.

Influence change. Make a list of what you don't like about your company or your job. Now, ask yourself if these are issues you can help improve. Where can you influence or lead others to make positive changes? Where can your personal example make a significant difference in changing the behavior of others?

Do your homework. If you are still determined to leave and have thoroughly and honestly gone through the previous eight steps, do some due diligence on the marketplace. What companies align with my values? Where will my skills be valued? What companies have an inspiring vision? Go beyond Google or company websites; reach out to friends in your network and utilize business social media to connect with people inside these organizations to get a more realistic picture. You owe it to yourself to not neglect this critical step.

Apply this process to your own situation or utilize it in guidance you may give a friend considering a career change. There is no place for "blind leaps of faith" in the crucial area of careers, especially in today's economic environment. This is an important mindset to be in and one that often needs shifting while in transition.

Working in tandem with the nine-point checklist are two significant mindset shifts that will not only make this reflection process easier but also make you more effective professionally (and personally).

Practice self-awareness. It is a gift granted to very few, but the good news is, it can be acquired. Comparing your current behavior to your internal standards and values and acknowledging your strengths, weaknesses, and desires can help you in every aspect of your life. There are countless personality tests available—DiSC, Birkman, Hogan, Myers-Briggs, etc. Become an objective evaluator of your job performance, how your peers and company leaders perceive your work, and how you interact with others. If you're not sure, ask them. Remember that if you find yourself considering a career change every few years, the one obvious and constant thread through each change is you.

You touch it, you own it. More than a decade ago, I was vice president of recruiting for a national restaurant chain with close to 2,000 restaurants and more than $1 billion in annual revenue. We had a saying embedded in the culture: "You touch it, you own it!" In a nutshell, you were empowered to act like an owner. Even if you had little direct responsibility for a particular issue or problem, you were expected to act like you owned all of it. No excuses, no complaining, and no blaming others—just do what you could to achieve the goal or fix the problem. It taught me the valuable lesson of taking personal responsibility for my actions and doing everything in my power to make things better. I also learned the importance of influence versus control and how I could make positive change, even when I did not have direct authority. In what ways can you influence better results?

Let's be honest, there are absolutely legitimate reasons why people change jobs. This chapter is not meant to dissuade you from doing that, but it is intended to help you think through the decision a little more carefully. Maybe you will pause and reflect long enough to realize that you can make a positive difference by staying, that an honest and open conversation with your manager might open new doors for you, and by practicing better self-awareness you will recognize those areas you can improve upon.

Respected executive coach Dean Harbry, founder of Internal Innovations, had this to share: "The workplace is a great place for personal development as well as professional development. Moving to another job before attempting to resolve conflicts properly or engage in healthy debate pretty well assures us that we will face the same issues in our next assignment. Developing an owner mindset and enhancing our influence skills will help us stay in the game until a needed change becomes obvious."

You just might decide you are in a good job after all and that it's worth investing in rather than leaving for greener pastures...which may not be so green after all. However, to do this topic justice, we need another perspective from someone who routinely peers into a broad spectrum of work cultures. I sought out the insights of Phoenix-based Andrea Chilcote, CEO of Morningstar Ventures. Andrea provides business consulting services on a national level in the areas of leadership development, executive development, team performance, and personal change. Her no-nonsense, results-oriented approach is personal and unique to each organization and individual. Her experiences, keen observations, and track record of success on a national level have always impressed me, and I am grateful to have Andrea's involvement in the book.

Andrea, I am curious about the coaching work you do with business leaders around the country. Do you find that many of them are seeking a meaningful life? What are some ways they define it?

"In my experience, just about everyone is seeking a meaningful life, although many would not characterize it that way. Research tells us that "purpose" is a core driver of human motivation. While we can certainly find meaning outside of work, true engagement in one's job or career is often dependent upon a greater purpose for the work.

"I have clients who would describe themselves as 'mission-focused.' These are people who actively seek work that, for them, points to a tangible cause greater than themselves. Others simply get satisfaction from using their unique skills and talents every day, usually to better the lives of the people they lead or serve.

"My work as an executive coach and leadership-development expert affords me the wonderful opportunity of working with leaders who have very diverse needs. Through my firm, Morningstar Ventures, I work with people at many stages of their careers, often at key transition points. For example, right now I am working with a client whose mission is to maximize his contribution in his current role before retirement from a senior executive position. At the same time, I'm working with two high-potential young professionals at the beginning of their careers, helping them pursue work that, from the start, is aligned with their talents, dreams, and values."

As we both know, it is not always necessary to leave your job to pursue a more meaningful life, yet many people make this assumption. What is your response when you hear this from a coaching client?

"I respond by asking a series of questions, beginning with, 'What do you want?' I believe in the first chapter of this book you describe the 'nagging feeling that something is missing.' This unclear state of mind leads to an urge to 'do something.' The obvious thing to do is to change jobs or careers. And the danger is that the job is just a means or mechanism for fulfillment.

"'What do you want?' sounds like a simple question. But the problem often does lie in defining what we truly want. Sometimes what we say we want is just a means of getting to some higher-level, often unexpressed, goal. We get attached to the mechanism—a particular job—and we miss all of the beautiful opportunities before us.

"So the next question is: 'What will that get you?' If what a client says he or she wants is merely a different job or organization, this next question helps to elicit what I call the 'outcome behind the outcome,' or the real goal. Then leaving one's job is just a choice, one among many choices for pursuing the true desire. That true desire might be right under one's nose.

"While my coaching work is primarily focused on business and career success, I will never forget the impact those two questions had on the life a client several years ago. She was working with me to quite literally decide whether to stay in or leave an unfulfilling job. As it turns out, she was also trying to decide whether or not to stay in what appeared to be an unfulfilling marriage. By answering those two questions, she realized what she was seeking was actually there before her. She reengaged in her marriage and found what she was seeking. That was ten years ago, and she's happy today."

What role does self-awareness play in making career decisions like the ones we are discussing?

"It's everything. As a coach, I utilize instruments that help me assess clients' core drivers, productive behaviors, and the consequences of unmet needs. When discussing the results of these assessment tools, I'm often met by a blinding insight into the obvious. They themselves had not consciously considered these how these traits impact satisfaction in work (and life), but when faced with the data, they have a whole new world of choices.

"This question gets to a core philosophy I have gained through my experience in this field. When we seek and gain true self-awareness—and then make informed choices about our work and relationships aligned with acceptance of our unique talents, traits, likes, and dislikes—our lives are truly purposeful."

Andrea, what has had the most significant impact on the professional and personal choices your clients have made regarding their careers?

"Unfortunately, it can take a major life event to precipitate the soul search that accompanies getting clarity about what one truly wants and needs. Usually it's a surprise or something that appears negative on the surface.

"If I were to list the primary catalysts for change, they would be: the threat of failure in a role, layoff or other job termination, an illness, or a death of a significant other.

"People who are fundamentally resilient use these life events to reconsider what's important."

Can you offer candid advice to professionals who may feel trapped in their jobs who are longing to do more, give more, and achieve more in life? How should they assess and navigate this dilemma?

"My candor relates to my previous comment. Don't wait until the wolf is at your door to consider these questions of meaning and purpose.

"I think that sometimes we stay stuck because we're embarrassed to announce a change of plans. Or, the pain of staying the unfulfilling course is easier to handle than answering to friends and loved ones who question our motives but don't always know how to act as a true thinking partner.

"Change itself is not what we fear; it's the transition that we endure getting from here to there that's not for the faint of heart. Transition does not always require that we leave and start anew. It does require that we honestly examine our beliefs and desires and embark on the journey, one step at a time."

❖

It would be easy to assume that our passion for pursuing the meaningful life cannot be attained in our current job, and that is simply not always the case. It is indeed possible and making a change should be considered very carefully for all the reasons you have been given by me and the candid observations of Andrea Chilcote. If your definition of the meaningful life leads you toward more faith, serving others, and finding more time with family, it is quite possible your current job can be the appropriate platform on which to build a life of your choosing. If you determine after a period of time that the job and the culture of your company is the main obstacle and you can't make positive changes, it is certainly time to consider moving on.

Questions for Reflection

◇ Using the insight from this chapter, do I feel I can attain a meaningful life in my current job and company? Why or why not?

◇ What are the work challenges which are in my control and how can I best influence them to improve?

◇ Am I asking myself, "What do I want?" and, "What will that get me?"

◇ If I follow Randy Hain's advice in this chapter and make the lists he suggests, what does this information tell me? Am I better equipped now to move forward in pursuing the meaningful life?

chapter
TEN
The Role of Crisis

"How we deal with these challenges and moments of crisis can ultimately define our future. If we are not satisfied with our lot in life, what will we do to change things?"

Job loss, illness, divorce, death of a loved one, and financial woes are the usual suspects when we consider the definition of "crisis." In a broader definition we can also have a crisis of faith, deal with challenges to our religious freedom, or struggle to deal with significant emotional challenges from various causes. How do we respond when faced with crisis? Can something positive come out of these challenges? How does this impact our pursuit of meaningful lives?

Because of my profession, I have most commonly witnessed professionals either struggling with forced job transition or their desire to leave their roles in pursuit of a better position. Many of them would describe this transition as the catalyst that led to significant life changes. Picture your life on autopilot, with everything going according to plan and you are pulled out of your lethargy by sudden job loss. You recognize that you have an opportunity to pursue a new path (see appendix two). What will you do? This is the question so many people face in today's economy. And as we discuss in the next chapter, it takes courage to pursue your dreams and a life with meaning.

For insight and guidance on the role crisis plays in the pursuit of a meaningful life, I reached out to respected consultant Brandon Smith, who is a leading expert in workplace health and dysfunction. He is the founder of theworkplacetherapist.com—a resource dedicated to eliminating dysfunction at work, improving workplace health, and restoring a sense of optimism in the workplace. When Brandon isn't treating dysfunction as an executive coach and consultant, he can be found at Emory University's Goizueta Business School, where he teaches and researches on topics related to healthy workplace dynamics, leadership, and communication.

Brandon, I am curious about the role of "crisis" in the lives of the professionals you observe in the workplace. Do you see crisis as a potential motivator that can help someone achieve a more meaningful life? Is it also a potential derailer?

"Crisis in the workplace is nothing more than a forced reframing of who we are and who we choose to be. Whether you lose your job or you've become burned out at work, those crisis moments can lay the seeds for creating a more meaningful life because they beg the question: 'is this all?' But we have to be careful. Depression and old patterns can just as easily come as a result of a crisis. It is much harder to recreate oneself and claim the purpose that lives in us than it is to bury one's head in a pillow and declare injustice."

What are some of the more common forms of "crisis" or interventions you have observed among professionals?

"The most common crisis by far is the layoff. Being forced off of the hamster wheel triggers thoughts of 'what's next?' and, 'Is this all there is?' More subtle crises that can trigger rethinking one's career are stress and burnout, abusive bosses, and corporate politics. But don't overlook personal losses. I see a large percentage of professionals make dramatic life and meaning shifts after personal crises like divorce or the death of a loved one. Those life catalysts can be tremendously motivating."

What counsel would you give professionals about staying focused on achieving a meaningful life? How do they stay on course?

"Fundamentally, purpose and meaning are about asking 'why?' I counsel professionals to regularly ask themselves variations of the following questions at least annually:

— "Do you feel a connection to your 'customers' (who you are helping or serving)?

— "Are you meeting a need in the world you feel passionate about?

— "Would you be proud to include your career accomplishments on your tombstone?

"If they have answers to any of the above, they likely have meaning in their job. If they come up empty, a change is in order."

In your view is there a kind of "secret sauce" that the majority of professionals leading meaningful lives seem to possess? Do you see patterns or an eclectic mix of character traits and experiences?

"The good news is that I see professionals leading meaningful lives in all walks of life, from social service to corporate gigs, from entrepreneurs to government employees. What is true for each and every one of these amazing individuals is that they choose to frame their identity and meaning in their work. They did not nor do they passively wait for others to provide them with the answers. So for each of us, the question is there to answer. In our brief time on this earth, how has our profession made a difference in the lives we touch?"

Brandon's perspective is almost uniquely similar to mine in that our professions provide a rare opportunity to peek inside companies and have candid conversations with business people around the country. His views on crisis were enlightening and broadened my perspective on this subject.

In order to look more closely at the role of crisis, we need to consider the story of someone who has experienced it firsthand. Ellina Feldman is a professional in her mid-twenties who has already led a fascinating life by any standard. Born in the Ukraine to parents who emigrated to the U.S. to flee religious persecution, she and her family have thrived in the United States. She received her undergraduate and graduate degrees in accounting from the University of Georgia in 2008, but realized a few years after graduation that accounting was not her passion and that she had been pursuing what her *family* wanted, not what *she* loved. With great determination she has been pursuing a career in business consulting that will use her people skills and love of problem-solving. She has also been working on a book about her grandfather, who was a Russian soldier in World War II.

Ellina, I am excited to share a little of your story in this book and the role crisis has played in shaping your journey. Please tell me about some of the experiences that have influenced your pursuit of a meaningful life.

"As with most children, my entire perception of the world was initially crafted by the lives of my parents and grandparents. I was born in Kiev, Ukraine, in 1985, one year before the Chernobyl nuclear explosion. My family lived comfortably, or so we thought, in a Communist time. My grandfather reminisced, '…We were so lucky that we didn't know how lucky we were.' We had all the necessities to live a happy life—food, shelter, and a tight-knit family. However, scholastic and professional success for a Jew in anti-Semitic Ukraine was nearly impossible. When the Iron Curtain was lifted, Russian Jews began to realize there was a brand-new world of opportunity in America. My uncle, always a go-getter, told my parents and grandparents of a better life where their children would have no limitations. After my grandfather gave the go-ahead, my family embarked on the journey to America as religious refugees. That moment marked the beginning of my perception of a meaningful life—giving up everything to give your children a better life. I was three at the time, but I remember witnessing the hardships that my family endured in our trek to America. We traveled from mid-October through December 29, 1989, through Rome, Vienna, New York, and ultimately Atlanta. We came through an organization called HIAS (Hebrew Immigration Aid Society), who graciously provided us an apartment and other basics."

How did you view the meaningful life once you settled in America?

"As I grew older and progressed through my scholastic career, I thought a meaningful life meant the pursuit of the American dream in order to:

— "Justify my family's decision to leave their motherland.

— "Live up to the expectations I imposed on myself because of how my family raised me.

— "Provide my future children a life where I would never have to say 'no, we don't have enough money for you to follow your dreams.'

"For most people, family is the initial example of how to live a meaningful life. However, it takes many individuals a lifetime to define it for themselves. When my grandmother passed away, I started to ponder the purpose of life. I resolved that it is love. Thus, since my grandmother achieved love in every aspect of her life—love of her parents, spouse, children, and grandchildren—she had fulfilled her purpose. I was a freshman in college when I came up with this view in a philosophy paper. Though at the time I didn't understand, my professor challenged my view by asking, 'What about all the things in between?' He elaborated, 'I love playing music on my guitar, I love riding my bike to campus, I love teaching, I love taking a stroll through a beautiful garden, and I love a delicious home-cooked meal.' I waved his viewpoint off as insignificant and continued the pursuit of my degree (which I didn't love) and thought I simply was in between having the love of my parents, and waiting for the love of my future spouse.

"It wasn't until I was twenty-five that I began to understand what he meant. I was in a job that I didn't love, without a potential spouse to love, living in an environment that I didn't love (my parents' house). I grew up always planning for the future. I wanted to build a life where I could comfortably provide for my future family. I had taken myself out of the equation completely, thinking that I could always find time for my true passion through a hobby. After a year and a half at a large public accounting company, plugging away at my cubicle, I realized that I was not living the life I planned. I had no husband, no children to provide for, and no house to maintain. Essentially I had no reason to be pursuing a career that brought me no personal satisfaction. I realized that I needed to reincorporate myself into the happiness equation. I realized that I had no reason to be miserable while I waited around for the life I planned to come to fruition. I also realized that every minute of life is a gift from God and it no longer made sense to be miserable at any point in time. I decided to pursue happiness even if it meant temporarily not residing at the career pinnacle. I was willing to take a step back and redefine my career goals and myself. I started to consider that I needed to fill my life with things that made me happy. I needed to create love and happiness around me instead of waiting for it to just happen.

"Currently, I believe a meaningful life is simply a purpose-filled life with freedom to pursue love and happiness."

Your family came here to flee religious persecution. How does your faith impact your life now?

"As I mentioned earlier, my family came to America as refugees. The irony was that we knew we were Jewish because our country branded us as such; however we had no idea what 'Jewish' really meant. Nearly all practice of Jewish tradition in Russia was wiped out during World War II. Everyone was consumed by fear and devastation as the country lost twenty million lives. Despite our non-religious lifestyle, Ukraine treated us as outcasts. Employment applications started off with, 'What is line five of your passport?' Line five reads: 'Nationality.' All Jews, regardless of their country of birth were listed as 'Jew.'

"I grew up not going to synagogue nor really knowing what Jews believed in. I only felt Jewish when we lit the menorah (the proper mechanics of which we never confidently understood—Right to left? Left to right? With song? Without?), when all my friends were taunting me about not going to church and going to hell because of it, and when I was really bored on Christmas. My parents didn't know much about the concept of God, so we never brought up the topic. We were Jewish by culture, by tradition, and by a legacy of people who gave everything to defend their faith.

"I believe my lack of faith played a role in my journey to understanding life. I didn't grow up being taught to look at the world through a particular lens. I had an almost jaded view of religion and was averse to having anyone try to instruct me on how to live. However, now that I have opened my mind and heart to believing in a higher power, I understand how powerful faith can be. Faith is shaping the next steps in my career and life in general. Believing that you will ultimately end up where you need to be takes quite a bit of pressure off of worrying about if you are making the right choice. Faith is allowing me to peacefully accept and appreciate every opportunity, knowing that my path has already been written."

Why do you think professionals of any generation fail to take the plunge and do more, give more, and achieve more in life?

"After I left the public accounting firm and went on a two-month trip to Europe, I realized that many Americans are bound by reasons of why they 'can't.' Sure there are a million reasons why a huge change may be impractical, but there is a bigger risk of giving up 'what if?' In my travels, I met many professionals in their thirties and forties who gave up a steady job and took the plunge to redefine themselves and their careers. Previously trapped by a mountain of obligations and responsibilities, they decided that their will to live a happy life allowed them to overcome any obstacle. It starts with a belief in yourself that you are worth more, a desire to follow your gut, and an unyielding willpower to push forward no matter what."

What specific role did crisis play in your pursuit of a meaningful life? Has it altered your outlook on the world?

"Crisis has always shaped my perception of a meaningful life. From the age of seven, I grew up watching my grandmother suffer through chronic strokes. By the time I was ten, she was completely paralyzed with partial dementia. I believe I was lucky enough to understand that life was not about pursuing the material things that entertained the rest of my friends. I was not concerned with toys or clothes or cars. I was concerned with family and appreciating the small gifts of life.

"Recently, my boyfriend's cousin was murdered at the age of twenty-five. To me, that was the biggest wakeup call of all. I realized that tomorrow is not guaranteed, so I need to do everything in my power to seize today."

Ellina's powerful story and journey toward a meaningful life is inspiring and encouraging. Her life has been filled with challenges and crisis points most of us will not likely encounter, but I find hope in her ability to seek strength in her difficult past and look forward to a brighter future. Her life experiences and perspectives coupled with Brandon Smith's candid observations in the workplace give a broad and helpful understanding of the role crisis plays as a catalyst to a richer and fuller life on many fronts.

How we deal with these challenges and moments of crisis can ultimately define our future. If we are not satisfied with our lot in life, what will we do to change things? If we are beaten to our knees by a personal, spiritual, or job-related crisis, will we have the strength and courage to persevere and forge a better life in spite of our setbacks? Ellina finds the strength to positively go forward from her family's history, how she was raised by her parents, and her burgeoning faith.

Brandon shared insight into how workplace-related crisis has been the motivation for positive change in many of the people he has observed.

How will you deal with crisis in your life and how will it help you achieve the life you want to lead?

Questions for Reflection

◇ What have been the crisis points in my life and how have I dealt with them?

◇ Can I honestly say crisis has helped me grow in my desire to attain a meaningful life? Why? Why not?

◇ Ellina and her family overcame great adversity to reach America, and those experiences have shaped who she is today. How has my upbringing and past shaped me? What can it tell me about the journey ahead?

◇ In the interview with Brandon Smith he was asked what counsel he had for professionals seeking to lead a more meaningful life. He offered three questions. How would I answer each question? How do my answers affect where I am going in life?

chapter
ELEVEN
Courage

"I took a chance—the chance of a lifetime—and approached my leadership about leaving the organization in the capable hands of the leaders we had helped develop over the years."

Courage is a noble and virtuous concept that can often be elusive in our daily lives. People want to think they are courageous, but how many opportunities pass us by each day to make tough decisions, speak out boldly on behalf of great causes, and give generously of ourselves for the good of others? One of the underlying themes I repeatedly encounter in my conversations with business people who lead meaningful lives is their seeming abundance of courage in making the difficult choices to forge a path to a life that is different from the norm. *Status quo* is not acceptable for them, and they are willing to boldly pursue a different kind of life that meets some deep inner need as well as addressing other and greater opportunities to serve others in the world.

Seeking other perspectives on this subject, I shared my views on courage and the pursuit of a meaningful life with Amy Balog, an organizational and leadership consultant, coach, speaker, writer, and the founder of ConnextionPoint (connectionpoint.com). Amy's deep involvement with her Fortune 1000 clients gives her a unique vantage point to observe leaders and their teams. I was curious about the role courage played in the career and life decisions of the professionals she has observed.

Amy, thank you for discussing your views on courage and a meaningful life. What are your thoughts on courage as it relates to pursuing this kind of life? What have you learned about courage from the professionals you work with in your client companies? Where does it emanate from?

"Well, we are in difficult economic times, and I hear a good deal of despondent thinking these days—a great deal of worry. We all know the road of life can take some hard turns. We hope and aspire to the ideal and then reality steps up to burst the bubble. We've seen many bubbles bursting over the last decade.

"We face tough jobs, stressed-out workplaces, joblessness, health challenges, family heartaches, and all shapes of unwelcome circumstances. The common thread behind all difficult circumstances is uncertainty. In fact our whole country is living under a cloud of perpetual uncertainty that is generating this chronic head cramp of worry. Worry is a dark current running silent but powerfully in our lives; the constant flow of worry undercuts any foundation to live meaningfully and to walk out our purpose.

"We can't always easily change our circumstances but we can place the counterweight of courage against the force of worry, although not any kind of courage will do. Courage has to emerge from the right place to give us the strength to regain meaning in a worry-riddled life."

What do you mean by the "right kind of courage?"

"In my executive coaching work I have found that many folks source their courage from performance. They feel courageous when they are winning…hitting their numbers, exceeding in performance reviews, making the boss happy, bringing home the paycheck, meeting the family's needs—the list goes on. They feel courage based on well-controlled circumstances, and the voice of this courage sounds like this, 'I am performing to a certain standard, I'm just keeping my nose above the water, and as long as I keep this up, I'm good. I still matter.' The challenge comes when circumstances change and with it the performance requirements. The boss changes, the job goes away, the company changes; or worse, the family changes. Life changes along with the performance requirements we once depended on to feel successful and meaningful.

"Courage riding the back of performance falls away and we find ourselves feeling frustrated and vulnerable. And worried!"

What are the downsides to this kind of courage? What is the solution? The alternative?

"This kind of circumstantially bound courage is fleeting and temporary. Life loses its meaning and becomes a daily slog when circumstances aren't playing nice. Courage has to come from a solid place deep inside of us to truly enable us to find meaning in our lives.

"The most solid place possible to mine resilient courage comes from our faith and our ability to create vision. With faith we can see beyond circumstances and build an identity that the world can't steal from us. With faith comes the ability to discover our gifts. Instead of spending time focusing on what is wrong with us and what can't be done, we can focus on what is right with us and what is possible to bring to the world. Faith teaches us a new form of courage that inspires us to approach people and situations with a mindset of giving versus a mindset of performing.

"Faith is the master of courage. I know this as my faith came alive in one of the darkest seasons of my life. In that season, performance-based courage simply fell fully away and faith-based courage took its place. I took up his yoke and took off an old suit strapped to performance, ideal circumstances, and false hopes. This gift of courage allows us to find meaning even in the hardest turns life deals us. Courage based on faith and vision stands firm. Courage based on performance loses its footing."

So you have seen and experienced courage drawn from faith as the most lasting form of courage?

"Think about it. How many stories of heroic leaders can you think of where they withstood incredible adversity, repeated performance failures and yet still brought forward a vision? It is the classic hero's journey. You have this journey in you. Faith-driven courage helps us make it through difficult times and serves as a fuel line to vision.

"Vision brings momentum to the table and ignites positive energy in a new direction. We create options that didn't exist before. We can even do the unthinkable. We find inspiration witnessing other's choices to meaningfully step out in faith to bring a vision forward, even when the world stands against them with snarky skepticism and doubt. This journey is not for those who base their courage on performance."

How does someone discover and use this type of courage?

"If your life feels adrift and undercut with worry to a point that you can't remember the last time you felt any inspired meaningful momentum, it is time to take inventory and ask honestly, 'What is the source of my courage?'

"Embracing the right kind of courage transforms a life filled with empty worry chained to a never-ending series of performance moments to a full life filled with giving, purpose, and meaning. Isn't that worthwhile?"

Amy's thoughts were enlightening and opened my eyes to a form of courage I had not truly considered, but I knew on some level that she was on to something. Seeking more insight and a new perspective, I reached out to Karen Bennett, a former senior human resources leader with a global Fortune 100 company who recently left her role to strike out on a new career and life path. You may wonder why I have included another HR leader in the book. I feel that professionals like Karen who have dealt with others looking to lead meaningful lives from their HR perspective and who have also experienced the challenge of this journey for themselves have incredibly valuable insight. I wanted to include her story as a great example of courageous decision-making and how to take a calculated leap of faith for the right reasons.

Karen, I am always curious how business professionals define a "meaningful life." What is your opinion?

"The opportunity to be present and enjoy every segment of my life is when it feels at its most meaningful: the areas of friends, family, health, work, community, recreation, new experiences, and connections with people are all being fulfilled. The people or things that are important to me are not neglected.

"What brings meaning to my life is making connections with others that somehow makes a difference, no matter how slight or how great. That I have been touched or have touched someone in a way that is remembered positively gives me the feeling of comfort and meaning."

Karen, I have heard you describe how important it is to be a good example to others and letting people know they matter to you. How do these fit into the meaningful life discussion?

"To dive a little deeper into this, I think of how it matters to me that I am a symbol of encouragement and motivation for the people in my life to want to be their best self. For my nieces and nephews, it is about instilling in them their value in this life and the criticality of the decisions they make that affect their character and integrity. For my siblings, mother, and grandmother it is about honoring the roles they have each uniquely played in my life and how that has helped to shape me as the person I am. For my friends, it is acknowledging the extended family they are and the gratitude I have for their lasting friendships. *Telling* people how they have influenced your life is probably the greatest gift I feel one can give, and I try to do that often."

It took a lot of courage to walk away from your successful career as a senior executive at a global company. What was your decision process in deciding to leave? What was the plan?

"I believe courage is the single word that describes what I did. I honestly think this was the single-most courageous thing I have ever done. And it didn't come as a quick decision. There is an expression that things 'happen gradually, then suddenly.' I think that fits my situation. As I look in the rearview mirror, I recognize my internal struggle to find 'what's next' for at least two years before I took this action. I placated myself and ignored this feeling by involving myself in more, diverse activities to keep me occupied and feeling like I was making a full contribution to life ('to whom much is given, much is expected' has sort of always been a mantra for me). So I became involved with many professional and community boards, even holding chair and officer roles in them. I enrolled in an executive MBA program. All of this at the same time I was holding down a pretty substantial executive set of responsibilities. It kept me occupied, overextended really, and unable to listen to the nagging voice inside questioning 'what's next.' And it worked for close to three years.

"Then, as my executive MBA program was coming to a close, culminating in a two-week international trip by the cohort, I had many hours alone with my thoughts on airplanes bringing me back from Asia to home. There are only so many magazines, meals, and movies that can occupy one on a seventeen-hour flight. And so the thoughts began: 'What's next?' This was followed by the sinking feeling that I knew that my job and I had enjoyed a wonderful relationship for over a decade, but that it was time to move on. Someone had said to me, 'Are you playing to win in your job, or playing not to lose?' Ouch! But it was such a true statement. I fought the feeling; I tried to hype myself into possible challenges that would still invigorate me. I found one: the installation of an HR shared-services center that I had recommended to the organization for years which looked as if it might gain support this time. This, I decided, would be the challenge that I wanted to see through. I promised myself once it was done, I would find a way to move on to my next chapter.

"The launch of the center was anticlimactic. My work was done. The next generation of leaders at the company would be well-prepared to revise and amend the work of the center as needed to reflect the changing needs and times of the organization. Would I go through with my commitment to 'move to my next chapter,' or would I chicken out?"

Did you move on to that next chapter?

"Yes. I took a chance—the chance of a lifetime—and approached my leadership about leaving the organization in the capable hands of the leaders we had helped develop over the years. It was a sort of 'out of body' conversation in that I felt I was watching myself (in disbelief) lay out a proposed plan to reorganize the department with a role like mine removed. I walked away from the conversation somewhat startled at what I had proposed, yet I had a complete sense of internal calm and closure all at the same time."

It would be easy for people to think this looked easy for you, but I know how difficult it was to leave your job. How meaningful has this time been for you?

"I say it over and over: This time of 'sabbatical' is truly a gift, and I try to honor it accordingly. Specifically, I am much more conscious and deliberate about being engaged in the segments of my life that are most important to me. The adage, 'I make plans, God laughs,' is probably the best quip I can offer about this time off. You see, life is unfolding in ways I couldn't have imagined, and by having this time available, I am able to dedicate my time to the things important to me. For example, I have been able to arrange for and be very involved in the care of my precious ninety-five-year-old grandmother, thanks to this gift of time. It has allowed me to spend much more quality time with her despite her rapidly advancing dementia; it has also given support and relief to my mother, her primary caregiver, which has helped evolve our relationship beyond mother and daughter to two women supporting one another through life's tough times. I was able to take my niece on her first tour of prospective colleges, affording me the precious time to spend with her and saving her parents taking the time off work to do these initial visits. In short, I have been where it seems I was meant to be without any internal conflict or struggle that I let my work always create inside of me.

"I stay current on my profession and the business community by continuing to hold professional board positions, attend business seminars, help consult with small businesses, mentoring in the business community, and continuing to cultivate the relationships I have been fortunate to make over the years.

"I have committed to myself to remember these lessons and the value of focusing on what brings me the most joy in my life and to not let go of it when I reenter the workplace in my next chapter."

What lesson(s) from this last job will you take into the next role?

"The most direct and honest way I can say this is that I simply knew I was not getting the joy from my work that I once did. I knew it for some time but felt there was no alternative...that you just had to keep keeping on. So I 'augmented' until my plate runneth over. And yet I was no happier. In fact, I was simply unhappy *and* tired!"

You were very strategic in making the decision to leave and start fresh, yet this can be intimidating for many. What advice would you offer others in similar career situations?

"I would encourage others in the same situation to be strategic in contemplating what they want next—whether it is at their current company or elsewhere. You can't just 'jump out' of your career without some sort of safety net. Honor your emotions, but don't let them be the primary driver of your actions. Take the time to assess honestly what you like about your current situation and realize that you won't be happy in the next one if you ignore these things. Even if they are a little embarrassing to admit (importance of job title, perks, perceived status the job brought you, the pride in the position you hold, etc.), this is the perfect time to evaluate what is truly important to you and what seemed like it was before you began to question staying in your role. Plan, cultivate (or maintain) your professional network both inside and outside of your company. The time to rely on a network will come when you make the leap to do something different, and if you have not made the efforts along the way, it is awfully presumptuous that it will be there to aid you once you are in need."

Karen, what prevents other professionals from making necessary and sometimes courageous decisions about their careers in the bigger context of pursuing meaningful lives?

"I think we all get caught up in the moment and the cadence of our careers, making little time (or priority) to reflect on what it is providing for us beyond the paycheck and lifestyle. But everyone is entitled to create a meaningful/purposeful life on this planet, and for most of us, it is hard to argue that the end all be all for this is work. As I said before, I believe a meaningful life encompasses all of the facets that bring you joy and satisfaction in being your fully realized and authentic self. Sometimes, we are operating from a place of crisis or survival and lose sight of this!

"Live your life true to your values and priorities, not those that anyone else may impose or suggest to you. Going through life with the 'mask' that jobs, society, social class, or the poll of public opinion may make you feel you must wear is not sustainable. So much wasted effort goes into fulfilling what we think others expect of us versus what we know as truth for ourselves."

Tell me what this stage of life looks like for you today.

"It is a time filled with immense gratitude and humility. I have made the time to reflect on the life I have led, the successes and failures that have shaped who I am, and the commitment to learn from these things so that I shape the next half of my life focused on what brings me joy and meaning. I feel strong, courageous, empowered, humble, and excited (versus anxious) to know there are unknowns that will come my way, but that they are part of what is to be my own personal journey."

Karen's story is filled with helpful lessons. She focused intently on her career and rose to the top of her profession. She recognized that she was running out of challenges and risked being bored in the future, so she developed a new group of leaders who would eventually replace her and executed a strategy to make her transition possible. This was about her timing, her decision, her vision...and her courageous decision to take the leap into the unknown. She is confident of her future and uninhibited in her pursuit of a new kind of life that makes her happy and offers the new kinds of challenges she seeks. It is interesting to note that Karen was continually growing and developing herself throughout her career, and this was one of the motivators for the courageous decision she made to seek a new challenge elsewhere. In essence, she outgrew her position. I also know she made the kinds of prudent financial decisions to be able to do this, and that can't be ignored, but her discernment, planning and courageous decision are worth considering if you find yourself in a similar place in your career.

Consider the possibility as well that you may make the courageous decision to stay in your organization and seek new opportunities and challenges internally as we explored in chapter nine. Courage does not always involve leaving and you will want to consider developing a game plan for your future growth and discussing it with your leadership team. More often than not, you will be surprised at the welcome response you will receive for proactively addressing your professional growth and future contributions to the organization with a well-developed plan.

Here is the bottom line: Evaluate where you are in your career, understand what you are seeking in your life, develop a game plan to get you to the right place, and have the courage to carry it out.

Questions for Reflection

◇ With all of the various forms of courage to consider, are there any I consistently exhibit? Any I lack?

◇ What are some key points in my life and career when I made courageous decisions? How did these decisions make me feel and what was the outcome?

◇ Am I continuing to grow and develop in my job? Do I see a point in the future where I will no longer be stimulated or satisfied with the work I am doing? Am I there now? Do I have a strategy to address this issue?

◇ Amy Balog shared: "The most solid place possible to mine resilient courage comes from our faith and our ability to create vision." Do I agree with this? Why or why not?

chapter
TWELVE
Getting a Do-Over

"The wise and fortunate ones are those professionals who intentionally and purposefully plot a course of action that takes them in the right direction."

You know somewhere along your journey you got off track. You may not know how or when it happened, but the realization dawns on you that something is out of alignment and you are not pursuing a life filled with meaning and purpose. In fact, you feel like you are living another life altogether.

I have experienced this firsthand and have observed it in my interactions with countless other professionals over the years. The sad fact is too many of us either don't know we are off track or we are off track and make excuses about why we do nothing about it. The wise and fortunate ones are those professionals who intentionally and purposefully plot a course of action that takes them in the right direction. They embrace change and seek opportunities that encourage happiness, intellectual stimulation, and service to others.

I reached out to two distinctly different professionals to interview for this chapter: Curt Johnson and Stephanie Tamargo. Curt is a marketing and business-development executive with active clients at consumer product, retailer, and restaurant chains throughout the United States. He is the president and founder of Blue Fire Marketing Group, which he founded in 2012 after a long and successful career in agency and corporate retail marketing and business-development roles.

Curt, thank you for taking some time to discuss your career choices as you pursue a meaningful life. What do you deem as important on this type of journey?

"After I transitioned out of what I believe is my last 'job,' I took a tremendous amount of time to think about this topic. Before this point, I didn't have time, or better said, didn't *make* the time to truly set my values and goals toward a 'meaningful life.' For me it comes down to these five things:

— "Connect with family and friends on a continuous basis—it should be a balanced work/life connection in your life!

— "Strive continuously for good health—this is a lifestyle, not meeting a doctor's requirements.

— "Generate more income in a smarter, more efficient way—control the situation!

— "Love and be passionate about someone and something—this drives everything in your life.

— "Believe in whatever *your* higher authority or spirit is, which allows you and others to believe in hope, love, purpose, and overall well-being and happiness. The happiest people I have found in my life are those who have the right balance for *themselves* of physical, mental, and spiritual."

You have been very intentional about your career, gaining agency and then corporate experience and now building your own consulting business. When did you know where you were headed? What was the motivation for these decisions in your life?

"I think all people who are self-driven have some form of historical catalyst. If you interview the greatest scholars, athletes, or artists, most will tell a story how they either overcame some overwhelming obstacle or they were destined—they knew from a very early age what they were going to be when they grew up.

"For me personally, it was a combination of factors. First, I didn't feel I was connecting at home as much as I potentially could be. When you are taking direction from someone else, you are not fully in control of your life, money, or success.

"Second, I was sick and tired of being inefficient throughout my day. I drove seventy-four miles a day to sit in an office, was needlessly interrupted frequently by other people about how they should do their jobs, and then have to get in the car, drive back home in awful traffic and pretend to be upbeat and satisfied in front of my family. These activities do not tie together very well.

"Third, I knew in my heart in July 2012 what I wanted to do. I talked to family, many friends, old mentors who worked in consulting and new mentors who were entrepreneurs. They all said the same thing—'I think you know what you want to do'. From then on, it was just a matter of convincing myself and my wife, then setting a few simple goals, and executing on these goals!

"What most people don't understand is the power of the human brain. We can, within reason, accomplish anything we set out to do. The keys are writing down what we want to accomplish and internalizing these goals so they are singularly focused. Nothing else matters."

Did you have doubts about making this work? What were the obstacles to you making the changes you have made in your career to get back on track... and how has the change been going?

"I did have some doubts, especially early on while starting a business. Can I do this? Why couldn't I be as successful as I wanted to be in someone else's organization? Will I fail? How long will this last? These are still questions in my mind, only much less.

"The key is confidence in yourself and, as you build the business, confidence in others to accomplish the company's goals. The other obstacles are easier to overcome—time and money. These will take care of themselves as long as you have the confidence and you believe in yourself and your mission."

What is important to you now versus fifteen years ago? Is this change in your life getting you back on track to achieve your personal goals?

"This move has absolutely addressed the goals I have long had but often ignored because of the career track I was on. Here is what is important to me today:

"Time: for family and for solitude.

"Health: preventative health every day so I can spend as much time on earth as possible with my family.

"Joy: creating fun and happiness through a better, more controlled life."

How do you fit in your family, faith, community involvement, and a brighter future into how you approach your daily work?

"That's easy because believe it or not, I have more time to focus on the things that are important to me!

"I have gained ten hours per week not commuting to and from an office and cubicle.

"I am not as tired when I get 'home' so I can be a better dad and husband.

"I have more confidence in myself so I can lead in the community and my faith.

"Simply put, I can be a better person!"

Stephanie Tamargo is a bilingual professional from the millennial generation who graduated in 2009 and is currently an account executive with a national advertising and marketing agency. She recently recognized that her life was "off track," and she is seeking to make some changes in her life that more closely align with her personality, interests, and values.

Stephanie, most professionals I have interviewed for this book have significant work and life experience. I am impressed with your desire at this early stage of life to be focused on a life filled with meaning. What does living a "meaningful life" mean to you?

"From an early age, I've always found myself aiming to live a meaningful life, but it wasn't until after I got into a life-threatening car accident at age eighteen that I truly understood what that meant. My desire was to live a full life; to ensure I was living every day as if it were my last, which to me just meant showing love to those around me and to be sure I was leaving a good mark wherever I was.

"Now, as an adult in the working world and as a woman who is engaged to an incredible man, 'to live a meaningful life' means something a little different now, too. It comes with having a healthy balance, where without a doubt, I place God and my family first, always. It means making sure I'm fulfilling my role as a woman preparing for marriage and hopefully, some day, as a mother.

"Working in my industry can feel redundant, and truly at the end of the day can oftentimes leave one feeling empty and dissatisfied. I yearn to do something for the betterment of humanity and the world. As I mentioned earlier, I've always had this search for more, but while I'm blessed with being alive, I want to make sure I'm living a life I'm proud of. Living a meaningful life means doing something that doesn't make me feel empty but rather gives me a sense that I'm doing something valuable that will leave a lasting mark in this world. Although I still have not found 'it,' I trust that through prayer, meeting different people, and my own research, I am certainly closer to finding what I am seeking."

Tell me about the influence of family and faith on the path your life has taken. Do you feel like something is missing in your life? Even though you are early in your career, does this feel like a "do-over?"

"I grew up in a family where the importance of faith and family was always clear and evident. My family certainly provided the foundation to shape my mentality, and I am grateful, as that mindset has stuck with me to this day. I can especially appreciate this now, as I prepare to begin my own foundation.

"I find that I am constantly striving and searching for something more, even though I am not missing anything in particular. In fact, I have everything I *need*: God, my family, good health, and life, but I'm always looking for ways to grow and change for the better. The journey for me is in searching for God's will for my life and even in the mistakes I make along the way. My faith allows me to see it this way and it is the underlying reason as to why I live my life the way I do. I suppose it does feel like a do-over now that I think about it."

Do you feel that people sometimes "settle" and put their values and dreams aside in order to grow their careers? Why?

"Most definitely. In today's world, there's no doubt that there's a great importance put on one's career and professional success. I feel as though people have forgotten about what matters most in life. It's not just about making ends meet, but our society defines the 'norm' via success, and success is defined by more money, more responsibility, rank at a company, a new car, a big house, the time spent traveling, etc. Yet at the end of the day, so many people who have such things claim that they feel empty—they, too, are searching for something more.

"With so much time focused on these things, people end up putting their families second and struggle to find the time to do other things. True priorities are so often shifted, set aside, or even ignored. Communication is lost between couples, parents, and their children;

family time is lost and the example is passed along to the next generation. It's become the new paradigm, one that we should avoid adopting.

"I have noticed how it is frowned-upon when a man or woman chooses to leave his or her workplace to stay at home with children. Although in reality, the values of this family are just countercultural and should be praised.

"If more time was spent focused on the things that matter most—on the people we love and call our family, on our relationships with people, on taking time to reflect, to take a step back from work—we may actually find peace and joy. If this were the case, I am sure that the world would be filled with happier, more fulfilled people."

What are some of the ways you keep your life and goals on track?

"Every few weeks, I try to take some time to reflect—usually while at eucharistic adoration—and write in what I call my prayer journal. It's a great way to put my thoughts down on paper while simultaneously praying to God. Whether I write about my current achievements, struggles, thoughts, fears, or questions about life, it's a great way of keeping a memoir of different times of my life. It also helps to hold me accountable because it's not just a thought in my mind, but it was significant enough to make me want to write about it, which allows me to realize that I need to offer these things to God. What I love most about having these things in writing is that I am able to look back through my journal and see what I have overcome, what answers I have come across over time, and how God has led me to new discoveries."

Curt and Stephanie, two professionals from different generations, share the same passion and desire to attain meaningful lives. Both are passionate about pursuing meaningful lives. For Curt, he is getting his life back on track after experiencing what life was like out of balance with his priorities out of order. Stephanie is self-aware enough to know that she is not where she needs to be and is determined through her faith and a passion for helping others to find the right fit for her life. She is also very focused on balancing those aspirations with her desire to be a wife and mother in the future.

What can we learn from Curt and Stephanie and perhaps others we have observed over the years about undergoing a "do-over" and getting our lives on track?

◇ It is never too late or too early in our lives to pursue this goal.

◇ We must be honest with ourselves about what is important to us and what we want out of life. Living in self-deception will result in a life half-lived.

◇ Personal happiness, faith, quality time with loved ones, community service and our health are all aspects of a life on track.

As we discussed in the last chapter, courageous decisions will be required.

Questions for Reflection

◇ Do I need a do-over? Considering the examples of Curt and Stephanie in this chapter and others I may know, what does a life on track look like for me?

◇ What are the likely signs of a life that is out of alignment? Do I see these signs in my life? In others around me?

◇ Stephanie made a clear point in her interview about "settling." Have I settled? If so, why have I settled?

◇ Curt took a long time and sought out the advice of mentors and candid friends before he made his decision to get his life on track and start his own business. What would this decision process look like for me? Who would I seek out for counsel about making an important life decision?

chapter
THIRTEEN
Intentionality and the
Paths We Choose

*"While always preparing for the unexpected, Tim's approach lessens
the negative impact of the unpredictable and maximizes
the potential good of that which is known."*

We have examined several aspects of the meaningful life in this book and hopefully been inspired by the candid insights of professionals from various backgrounds and areas of the country. All of them have defined the meaningful life for themselves in different ways. Some of them focus on the importance of faith and family. Others have a passion for serving others, and some simply want to do work they love. Whatever your background, I truly hope you have found this eclectic mix of experiences and views helpful in providing a guide for your own journey.

As we wind down our exploration of the meaningful life, I feel it is important to share the story of one more business person whose journey toward a life filled with meaning and purpose may just be the most intentional I have ever known. From an early age, Tim Tassopoulos has been driven by goals and a clear vision of the exceptional life he is determined to lead. Although too humble to describe himself this way, I can assure you that Tim is a man who lives a life in full and is a wonderful example to those blessed to know him.

Tim, a member of the Chick-fil-A executive team, is the executive vice president of operations at Chick-fil-A, which he joined as a team member in 1977, and is responsible for coordinating the activities of field operations and a number of other departments across the organization. He is also a proud husband and father, a man of strong faith, a mentor, and a tireless servant of the community. Some of his favorite service commitments are teaching the high school Sunday school class in his church, volunteering with the Boy Scouts, and serving on college boards. In my opinion, Tim is the epitome of the "servant leader." I was grateful that Tim took time out of his busy schedule to discuss the book and his thoughts on achieving a meaningful life.

Tim, I have been looking forward to gathering your thoughts and experiences for the book. What does living a meaningful life look like to you? How do you stay focused on attaining this life?

"My immediate reaction is 'what do I give versus what do I get?' What is my contribution to the world and what difference have I made? What am I doing with what God has given me? God gave me the gift of life and my gift back to him is my life. In a nutshell, how I measure and define my life is how I think about these questions.

"I am extremely goal-oriented. I have broken down my weekly goals to the 'Four Circles,' which are the areas of God, Family/Friends, Professional, and Community. I address and plan my goals around these areas every Sunday night, which helps me focus on honoring God, growing my impact with my family, and investing in my work and the community. I also consistently review and update my life plans and consider how factors like my circles of influence and the rhythm of time play a role in my goals."

You have been very intentional about the path of your career, spending time with your family, and serving your community. When did you know where you were headed in life? What were the catalysts in your early years for the decisions you have made in your life?

"Four things come to mind immediately:

1. "My parents were very encouraging and supportive, and this made a tremendous difference in my life.

2. "My key experiences in high school:

   — "When I was in high school, I was not that goal-oriented.

   — "I had a great teacher in my senior year of high school who really invested in me and inspired me.

   — "I felt challenged and motivated to do my best after being with fellow graduates at high school graduation.

   — "I worked for a great operator as a teenager when I started with Chick-fil-A named Gary. He helped me to start writing detailed goals and developing an intentional life planning process. I learned to understand 'why' I am doing 'what.'

3. "I got married! As much as I wanted to start the goal-setting process with my wife, I found that I am more goal-oriented with a big emphasis on written plans, while Maria is more relationship-oriented, with an emphasis on one-on-one connections. Our focus from the beginning has been more about our family and future, while individually we respect each other's different approaches.

4. "The Chick-fil-A environment and culture attracts people who are 'purpose-filled.' I remember one of my CFA mentors named Jimmy from years ago who always expected the best from me and taught me to ask the same from those around me."

What obstacles have you faced to living a life with meaning, and how have you overcome them?

"This is a great question, and to be honest, I have ongoing struggles in several areas. Here are three that are frequently on my mind:

1. "*Selfishness.* I wrestle with 'it's all about me vs. leading a meaningful life.' To keep me on the right path, I look to the role models in my life who are not challenged by this problem and to my relationship with God.

2. "*Busyness.* It makes me lose focus, get distracted, and I have a difficult time saying no. How do I overcome this? I work on being more intentional about staying God-oriented in my thinking and actions. I stay focused on my goal-setting and planning.

3. "*Inauthentic relationships.* I know I must stay focused on the wholeness and growth which come from good relationships. Finding and maintaining authentic relationships is about staying in the moment with someone and being present. It is about intentionally thinking about others and their goals. It is also about connecting my desire to be 'other's focused' to something real."

Tim, you have an admirably long tenure with the same company, which is very rare these days! What role does culture and environment play in your decision to stay committed to the same company? How has working for Chick-fil-A helped you on your journey?

"I have been with CFA for more than thirty-five years, so my work environment has had a tremendous influence on my own pursuit of a meaningful life. I can be my own worst critic at times, but overall I feel incredibly blessed and grateful for the place I am at right now. Chick-fil-A has specifically helped me in three key areas:

1. "Chick-fil-A is a principle-centered organization based on both biblical principles and those of our founder, Truett Cathy.

2. "Chick-fil-A has a clear purpose in the world. Our Purpose Statement says it all: 'That we might glorify God by being a faithful steward in all that is entrusted to our care, and that we might have a positive influence on all the people that we might come in contact with.'

3. "When Chick-fil-A or any team for that matter is at their very best, I see a leader who is highly personal and highly professional with a focus on clarity, connectedness, and results."

Tim, what would be your advice for anyone in business today looking to achieve career success, find balance, and serve the community on the way to a more meaningful life?

"*Be a student.* Have a learning and growth mindset and keep your ego in check!

"*Value relationships.* Pay attention to people who are closest to you. Be authentic! Be open to feedback. Ask, 'What is it like to be on the other side of me?'

"*Always wrestle with this question:* 'Is it what I give or what I get?' Remember it all comes back to you in the end."

So many people I have encountered over the years have had their lives influenced and shaped by factors out of their control. What Tim Tassopoulos offers is a path rooted in intentionality that helps him stay focused on his goals and the pursuit of a life filled with meaning. While always preparing for the unexpected, Tim's approach lessens the negative impact of the unpredictable and maximizes the potential good of that which is known. His perspective and example is important, but ultimately you must decide the process you will use to make the decisions that will determine your future.

Questions for Reflection

◇ How do I plan and make goals compared to Tim's approach? Are they providing me the results I desire? Why or why not?

◇ This chapter to some degree comes down to the issue of control. Am I exercising a beneficial degree of control over my life or am I being heavily influenced by factors outside of my control?

◇ Tim was candid in describing his key obstacles to leading a meaningful life. How do selfishness, busyness, and inauthentic relationships factor into my pursuit of a meaningful life?

◇ If my approach to a meaningful life is not getting the desired results, can I adapt to Tim's approach? Will I sit down each week and make detailed goals that help me understand "why" I am doing "what?" Who will hold me accountable?

chapter
FOURTEEN
Practical Steps

Over the course of *Something More*, I have been careful to not narrowly define exactly what the "meaningful life" is for you. As you have learned from the men and women interviewed in the book and my own observations, how people view this can vary greatly. It is my goal, however, to provide a logical framework and a practical road map to enable readers to begin their journey toward the meaningful life, as so many professionals over the years have shared with me that they simply need help getting started.

Here is a helpful checklist of what you will need on your journey:

◇ **Self-awareness.** Are you aware of your challenges and strengths? Do you have the ability and willingness to reflect on past actions and learn from your mistakes?

◇ **Important character traits.** As we learned in this book, the capacity for honesty, humility, transparency, passion, selflessness, authenticity, courage, and serving others will be important on this journey to a meaningful life. Do you possess these traits now and, if not, are you willing to work at developing them?

◇ **Candid friends or mentors.** Are there people in your life who are willing to speak truthfully to you about your life and hold you accountable?

◇ **Listening and learning skills.** Will you take the advice of trusted friends and make the necessary changes? Will you seek out people you admire and want to emulate so you can learn from them?

◇ *Flexible mindset.* Your willingness to be flexible and make the necessary changes in pursuit of a meaningful life is critically important.

Here is a framework you can use in the pursuit of a meaningful life:

◇ **Identify What Is Missing**

The first step is identifying what is missing in your life. At first it was balance for me, but I realized later that I was missing a relationship with Christ and the welcoming arms of the Catholic Church. What is missing in your life? Balance, faith, focus on health, serving others, a job you love, intellectual stimulation, outlets for your creativity, etc.?

◇ **Know Your Motivations**

What is the motivation behind your desire for a meaningful life? Nicole Siokis was able to identify her desire to be a great mother, her daughter's future, serving others, and building her own business as her primary motivations. Also, be wary of negative and unhealthy motivations such as insecurity, fear, blind ambition, and excessive pride, which can frustrate our desire to make good decisions in life.

◇ **Assess the Obstacles**

What obstacles stand in your way? It is important to identify these and have a plan to overcome them. In chapter three, Dr. Kirk Baxter, Dr. Karen Steadman, and Mark Newton identified frustration, self-doubt, lack of knowledge, lack of self-awareness, lack of discipline, feeling overwhelmed, stress, lack of boundaries, illness, economic conditions, and fear of failure as potential derailers on your path to a life filled with meaning and purpose. It is important to have people in your life to help you identify these obstacles if you are unsure.

◇ Change Your Mindset

At some point the path to a meaningful life will lead to a crossroads and difficult choices will often be required. If we fail to reorient our thinking (about our job, the need for balance, doing work we enjoy, etc.), we are likely to fall into the same harmful routines and never escape to a more meaningful life. Reflect on the example of Kimberly Samon in chapter four, who shared in great detail how her thinking evolved over time to help her reach the place in her life she is in now.

◇ Be Authentic

Authenticity is connected to the integrated life, but it is worthy of standing on its own. Being real in today's world can be challenging for a number of reasons including a lack of self-awareness, fear of not fitting in, fear of judgment, attachment to an income level that requires unhealthy compromises, and a lack of confidence. It is almost impossible to pursue a life filled with meaning if we can't be our authentic selves at all times. The examples of Beth Valenta and Richard Smith in chapter five, as well as countless others I have encountered, show the possibilities that await those who publicly embrace their real selves.

◇ Lead an Integrated Life

Have you gotten to the place where all the various pieces in your life are meshing well? Are you able to integrate your work, passions, family, faith, creativity, and the other things important to you seamlessly into your daily life and harness the benefit of being yourself and not multiple people depending on you environment? Tami Heim's perspective in chapter six of a foundation built upon faith and the way she leads an integrated life is a wonderful example to follow.

◇ Leveraging Our Gifts and Achieving Greatness

We all have gifts, but how do we use them? This is the key challenge addressed in my chapter-seven interview with Glen Jackson. His clear perspective is to always use your gifts, no matter how modest, in the service of others and to recognize that all gifts come from God. Dr. Paul Voss encourages us to consider the nature of greatness and recognize the greater value of excellence. Have you achieved greatness in any area of your life? Did you know that it is also "great" to be an excellent parent, loving spouse, selfless leader, good steward, faithful friend, dedicated employee, and to be blessed with strong faith?

◇ Recognize the Illusion of Success

What is truly important to you? How do you measure your own success? Is it the bank account, nice home, new cars, and keeping up with the neighbors? Through the examples of my own father and Andreas Widmer in chapter eight, we see two men who have looked past the illusion of success thrust upon us by the world and instead have learned to value more highly their relationship with God, their families, and giving back to the community.

◇ Should I Stay or Should I Go?

There is often an assumption that you must leave your job and find another before you can begin pursuing a meaningful life. Wrong. It is not always necessary to leave your company for the untried yet seemingly greener pastures in another organization. There is a process, as I lay out in chapter nine, to carefully evaluate this decision. The interview with Andrea Chilcote provides you the insight of someone who has worked with business leaders in diverse work cultures across the country for years. Her candid insights and tough questions to ask yourself will be invaluable as you travel down the path toward the meaningful life.

◇ The Role of Crisis

Family or personal illness, job loss, death of a loved one, divorce, financial woes, religious persecution, and emotional challenges are all real challenges that can reach crisis level for today's professional. Through Brandon Smith's perspectives and observations in chapter ten as a coach and business consultant dealing with workplace dysfunction as well as Ellina Feldman's gripping story of fleeing religious persecution in the Ukraine to settle in the U.S. and pursue her professional goals, we have seen how crisis can impact our pursuit of a more meaningful life in various ways and can happen when we least expect it. In some cases it can accelerate our journey and help us appreciate the meaningful life even more.

◇ It Takes Courage

Showing courage in the pursuit of a meaningful life is not always about leaving your job, although this may sometimes be necessary. Courage can be a number of things, and we examine some of them in chapter eleven through the interviews with business coach Amy Balog and senior HR executive Karen Bennett. Amy points out the need to focus on the right kind of courage and encourages us to not be "chained to a never-ending series of performance moments" and instead display our courage in the pursuit of lives filled with meaning and purpose. Through the interview with Karen Bennett, we hear the candid story of the planned approach to her successful career, driven by self-awareness and a desire for new challenges, and her courageous decision to leave it all as she considers the next chapter in her journey.

◇ Getting a Do-Over

Sometimes you get another chance with your career and can focus on living a meaningful life. Through the interviews in chapter twelve with senior executive turned successful consultant Curt Johnson and millennial account manager Stephanie Tamargo, we learn about two distinctly different journeys to reach the meaningful life. Curt had a very traditional and successful career in his industry but was making sacrifices in time with family, ignoring his health, and was unhappy. He decided to start his own consulting company and has felt reborn with all of the important areas of his life reenergized. Stephanie presented a different take as she is relatively new in her career, but is self-aware enough to know that her life is "off track" and she is seeking to make some changes in her life that more closely align with her personality, interests, and values. She also wants to focus more on her faith and have her career accommodate starting a family in the years ahead.

◇ Be Intentional

It is difficult to achieve your goals if you don't have a plan. Living a life filled with meaning requires a plan, but it also requires intentionality. All of the people I interviewed for this book have been intentional in their planning and actions, perhaps none more so than Chick-fil-A executive Tim Tassopoulos (chapter thirteen). From an early age, Tim has been focused on setting goals and planning how he will achieve them. This intentionality affects his successful career, the family he adores, the leaders and future leaders he mentors in his organization, and the numerous nonprofit groups who are grateful to have Tim's active involvement. Tim minimizes unpredictability with his approach and maximizes the potential good of that which is known.

Conclusion

A Man I Know

I lit a candle and prayed in our parish chapel not long ago for a man I know in his mid-seventies who is struggling with various health issues as he gets older. The candle I lit burned brightly, more brightly than the others, for the hour I was in the chapel. The light reminded me of his life filled with countless good examples and a wonderful legacy of lives he has touched. Let me tell you a little about him.

He had a challenging childhood. His father left when he was a little boy and he, his two brothers, and twin sister were raised by his alcoholic mother and grandmother. He made his way through childhood with no real fatherly influence and very little money to keep the household going. The man was good at sports and played high school football and focused on girls and going to the beach as ways to escape the emotional turmoil at home.

He joined the Army at age eighteen, and the military formed the basis for the man he became. He learned self-discipline, gained a work ethic, and became a leader. After six years he left to join the real world and started his career. He was very different from the rash teenager he had been and was now a mature man focused on starting a new life. He met and fell in love with a woman a few years later, and they settled down to start a family.

The happy couple had a boy, and both he and his wife were busy pursuing their careers and raising their child. He tried college, but after two years decided it was not for him and focused instead on working as hard as he could to support his family. The man turned out to be the opposite of his own childhood experience. Although he was not perfect, he always made time after work to play catch with his son and to teach him valuable life lessons. He loved talking to his son about the importance of getting a good education, working hard, helping others in need, and always doing your best. This hard-working father grew up in a generation that didn't easily show affection, and he was rarely heard to say "I love you," but his actions showed the depth of his feelings toward his family more than words ever could.

A daughter was born after they moved to Georgia in the early 1970s, and the family was complete. The years went by and the man started attending church at the urging of his wife. He found a true calling as a Sunday school teacher and faithful member of the church. The man and woman continued to raise their children and built a good moral foundation in the home and set great examples with their work ethic and devotion to family. The man was well-known in the community as a good friend, hard worker, devout churchgoer, selfless giver, good father, and husband.

He saw first his son and, years later, his daughter off to college. He had always placed a premium on education, and it made him very proud to see his children live out his dream. Disappointments and triumphs followed in the next several years as the man watched his children stumble, fall, and get back up again in their pursuit of life, love, and happiness. He just kept on working and giving testimony with his life, and his children could easily see a great example to follow, even if they didn't always appreciate him.

The later years saw the son raise a family of his own and the daughter get married, have a son, and get divorced. Out of his sense of duty and compassion, he took his daughter and grandson into his home with his wife and they helped to raise their grandson. He still taught the timeless lessons of a good work ethic, strong values, and education. His happiest moments always seemed to be a teaching opportunity with his daughter's son and the sons of his firstborn. The man's age, a life of hard work, and a smoking addiction he only gave up in 2008 have caught up with him, and he is dealing with various health challenges. Even when he is not feeling well, he always smiles and makes the conversation about you and not himself.

I wonder if he recognizes how many lives he has touched by the example of his incredible work ethic, making good moral choices, and always offering to give of himself to others—never asking for anything in return. He was married to the same woman for forty-five years until her death in February of 2010, and the dignified and caring way he handled her loss was another grace-filled example to emulate. I hope he knows how he has influenced me by the meaningful life he has led, and I look forward to telling him in person as soon as possible.

The man is known by several names: husband, brother, friend, Papa, and Steve. I have always just called him...Dad.

Dad, thank you for being the best example a son could ever want and for showing me how to pursue and live a meaningful life. I hope I pass along what you have taught me to my own children.

appendix
ONE
A Road Map for Effectively Serving on Nonprofit Boards

Over my twenty-plus years in business, I have had the good fortune to serve on a number of nonprofit boards and am grateful for the enriching experiences, people I have met, and worthy causes I have served. Because so much of this book is about finding a meaningful life by serving others, I want to share the lessons I have learned about how to effectively serve on a nonprofit board. In my earlier days, I wasn't aware there was a right and wrong to it. This appendix seeks to cull this information into an easy-to-follow road map that will hopefully enrich your board service experience and help add value to the organizations you serve.

"Why should I serve on this nonprofit board?" It's the fundamental question we should ask ourselves before accepting a board position. Our time is stretched thin and free minutes are precious, so evaluate any extra time commitments with thoughtful discernment. I recommend reviewing the following questions as part of the evaluation process:

◇ What is the reputation of the organization in the community? Is the leadership team effective? Can I speak with references and existing board members?

◇ How often does the board meet, and what is the time commitment required of board members?

◇ Does the board have D&O (directors and officers) insurance?

◇ What will I have to sacrifice personally and professionally in order to give this organization what it requires of me?

◇ Do my passions and interests align with the mission of the organization?

◇ Will my skills and experiences help me be effective on the board?

◇ Am I willing to champion the cause of this organization to my network and potentially ask for donations?

◇ Is there a minimum personal donation required of board members?

In my first board role more than fifteen years ago, I was so excited to be invited that I didn't ask many questions. Even though the mission of the organization aligned with my passions and interests, I quickly learned that the nonprofit had a dysfunctional leadership team, a poor reputation in the community, and they desperately needed me to help them raise money. It was a painful lesson for me, but I learned from it.

Making a Difference or Padding a Résumé?

Ask yourself if your desire to serve on a nonprofit board is to truly make a difference or build your résumé. I have worked alongside both types of directors. The people who have a heart for service add significant value and find their experience rewarding. People wanting to serve for the sake of appearances can have a negative effect on the organization by not contributing at the expected level and taking the seat of someone who is willing to be active.

Innovative Ways to Add Value

Did you know there are other ways to help the organizations you are serving besides writing a big check? While individual contributions are helpful, we may not always be in a position to provide significant personal resources. I have helped develop alternative ways to provide value to the nonprofits I have served. Here are a few proven ideas:

◇ **The small gathering.** Host a small, intimate gathering in your office or at a restaurant of other business leaders to hear a guest speaker present on a relevant topic. This can be an author, recognized business leader, or a professional service provider offering views on the market or trends. Invite the head of your nonprofit organization and make introductions. Provide a meal in a relaxed setting and invite people who have a heart for giving back. This approach creates more awareness in the business community for the nonprofit, attracts potential volunteers for the organization's projects, and draws potential donors.

◇ **The forum concept.** This is a modification of the above idea, but think bigger. Every six months my firm hosts a Bell Oaks Forum, usually in partnership with a local university, at one of their facilities. We invite 100 to 150 senior business leaders to hear someone of interest present on a relevant topic. We usually select a nonprofit our firm supports as a "community sponsor," place its logo and information in our marketing materials, and recognize it at the forum. We invite the organization's leader to say a few words and offer a place for it to distribute marketing information. The events are free, and we invest in coffee and a light breakfast for the attendees. Everyone involved—the speaker, attendees, presenting organization, and nonprofit—benefits.

◇ **Gifts that matter.** Every Christmas, many of us give generously to our clients and business colleagues to whom we wish to show our appreciation. Next year, instead of giving the overstuffed gift basket or box of cookies, make a donation on their behalf to your favorite nonprofit. Each year our firm makes a donation to our favorite causes in the name of clients and friends; the response has been wonderful and we are able to help in a meaningful way the causes we support throughout the year.

◇ **Open your network.** Actively introduce key business leaders and other valuable resources to the leaders of the nonprofits you serve. If you are aware of their organizational needs, you may be able to get friends to donate their skills and professional services *pro-bono*, which is of enormous value. These coffee and lunch meetings you facilitate can often produce a lot of positive results for both parties, and it is as simple as sending an introductory e-mail.

◇ **Promote, promote, promote.** Use e-mail and social media to promote the nonprofits you serve. Social-media updates on upcoming events for your nonprofits can help raise their profile in the community. Send updates to your network when the organization is in the news or if any of the leadership is quoted. This is incredibly valuable and costs a minimal investment of time.

Things to Avoid

As much as this is about things to do, I also want to address what to avoid when serving on a nonprofit board. Here are few observations and experiences:

◇ **Don't overcommit.** Be prudent when volunteering for a board or committee assignment.

◇ **Don't be impatient.** Nonprofits don't typically run like our companies and they are not supposed to. Process, deadlines, and growing revenue can be alien concepts.

◇ **Don't forget to "experience" what the nonprofit is all about.** Don't serve on a board and fail to get personally involved in its mission. Get out in the field and help! You can't sell what you haven't experienced firsthand.

◇ **Don't ignore the need to build collaborative friendships on the board.** You will be relying on each other in the future to get things done, so meet your fellow board members. I have made some incredible friendships through my board service.

I am a better person because I give time to serve nonprofits in our community. As I have gotten older, I have become keenly aware of what causes I am passionate about and what I have to offer. My hope is that this road map will help you maximize your own board experiences and make a meaningful difference in the community. We have much to offer. These organizations need our help. Let's get started!

appendix
TWO
The Upside of a Job Search in a Down Economy

When faced with an opportunity to fundamentally change your life, will you take it? Many of us want to answer this question with a resounding "yes," but may think that reality is not attainable. Not necessarily so. Consider the possibility that the current economy may be providing the catalyst for meaningful lessons and positive life changes to people all around you.

In my profession, I meet dozens of business people every month, many of whom are professionals in transition. My interviews often take the form of an informal dialogue where I invite job candidates to share not only work experiences, but also how they are feeling and coping with being out of work. The feedback has been illuminating. There are striking similarities in the challenges this group faces after they leave their jobs, which fall into three distinct categories: relevancy, validation, and balance.

Uncovering the benefits of these three areas now can benefit your work and entire life for the long term. Life challenges have a way of forcing much-needed self-discovery, and what you learn can change your life. Now is the time to do it...we won't be in a tough economy forever, and your focus will be shifted elsewhere again. Here are some ways to do that.

Relevancy

The upside: It's never too late to start. It is a daunting new world for the job seeker today. As if the shock of losing a job is not enough, many candidates quickly learn that they have lost some degree of relevancy while plugging away at their former jobs. They have neglected to maintain a network inside as well as outside their places of business. The latest online social networking tools are a mystery. Paradigm shifts in how to effectively reach prospective hiring managers are vastly different from the last time they were on the job market, and many have not remained on the leading edge of their industry.

So why is this important? Long tenures at companies are becoming a rarity. It is likely that you will experience multiple job changes over your career, and you need to be prepared for that eventuality. Staying well-networked in and out of your organization is critical. Just as important is the need to stay on top of new trends not only in your industry, but in the marketplace in general. The vast majority of job candidates I meet spend the first few months of searching in a steep learning curve attempting to become current and trying to frantically build personal and professional networks they should have been nurturing along the way.

The challenge of staying relevant is not necessarily generational. This issue affects everyone from recent college grads to seasoned professionals. Regardless of your position or years of experience, begin thinking beyond the silo of your current position (or next one) and make a commitment to be well-networked, well-versed on industry and market trends, and above all, relevant when you find yourself in career transition.

Ideas for Staying Relevant

◇ Build and maintain relationships by having coffee or lunch once a week with someone outside your organization. Do the same with colleagues inside your company.

◇ Make your personal and career development a priority. Read books and take courses relevant for your industry and for achieving your personal goals. Attend seminars, workshops, networking events, etc.

◇ Utilize social networking tools to manage what should be an ever-expanding network. Be visible!

Validation

The upside: There are healthier ways to feel good about yourself! Your boss says you're doing a good job. Clients thank you for delivering great service. Friends in the office tell you they respect your strong work ethic. You are respected in the community and appreciated at home as the person who has it all: great job, wonderful family, strong commitment to stewardship, and work/life balance. Each and every day carries with it some form of validation that is directly connected to your self-worth. Then you lose your job....

This loss of personal validation is rarely written about but often comes up in my discussions with candidates who have been out of work a month or more. At this point, reality has set in and often self-worth begins to be adversely affected. The hard lessons of a job loss force many to confront this uncomfortable reality, but there is hope.

Consider these alternate means of validation: "I love you, Dad," "Thanks for coming to my game, Mom, it means a lot to have you here," "I am grateful for your candid advice and appreciate your friendship," or "I really appreciate you helping out with the school play—we couldn't have done this without you." You get the picture.

The validation coming from family, friends, and your community can be much more meaningful. Your job should not define who you are....You don't want people to remember you with: "He sure had a great career!"

Executive coach and business consultant Brandon Smith several months ago suggested overcoming the challenge of loss of validation through the lens of finding one's purpose. He offered this insight:

"Perhaps the greatest antidote to the struggle job seekers face today with validation is purpose. Purpose connects us to the needs we are ultimately trying to meet in the world, either through our job or beyond. Purpose is critical in these times because it gives us a way to proactively make sense out of the world and see how the world needs us today more than ever.

"What a different orientation than most job seekers currently take. Rather than waiting to be seen for the value one brings, when we have a sense of purpose and lead with that during these times, it can allow us to approach companies and tell them how we can help them overcome their struggles today. It can also provide us a channel through which to get validation."

In other words, pursue your passion in your next job and not just a means of making a living.

Ideas for Regaining (Healthy) Validation

◇ Don't let your work define who you are. If you could write the story of your life, think about how you would make it full of family and friends whose lives you positively impacted.

◇ Brandon Smith offered this idea: "Consider your purpose. What need are you trying to meet today in the world? How might companies need you today more than ever? Consider using this to reframe your orientation and your approach to the job search."

◇ Pay it forward. Make the effort to help others during your search. Offer candid advice, help with networking, be a good listener.

Balance

The upside: You can rediscover what you should be working for. The most profound difference for many of the job seekers is the rediscovery of the joys of family. They are able to spend quality time with children and get reacquainted. The former drudgery of a heavy travel schedule is transformed into taking the kids to school and relishing every school activity and event. Reconnecting to spouses and reinvigorated marriages are often a result of this job hiatus as couples who only saw each other on weekends are actually required to communicate on a daily basis. Many speak of a newfound sense of community, and others talk of a deeper relationship with God. Often, people are finding the personal time they always needed (and never had) to get in shape through exercise and better eating habits. Their lives are coming into balance for maybe the first time in years.

Peter Bregman, CEO of a global leadership and change-management consulting firm, wrote an article for *Harvard Business Review* titled, "Need to Find a Job? Stop Looking So Hard." He suggests: "If you're passionate about what you're doing, and you're doing it with other people who are passionate about what they're doing, then chances are the work you eventually find will be more in line with the stuff you love to do. And then your life changes."

To be sure, there are significant stresses during a job search, especially financial pressures to find a new job quickly. But this respite from the storm is allowing a pendulum swing in a positive direction that many candidates are utilizing as a catalyst to pursue a career and life change. As they look for new jobs, they are intentionally focusing on roles that allow for greater work/life balance and less travel. Climbing the corporate ladder is increasingly taking a backseat to the pursuit of the more fulfilling roles as well-rounded husbands and wives/fathers and mothers.

As Brandon shared, pursuit of your purpose is important. In that context, ask yourself if your work exists to serve your family or if your family exists to serve your work. I have often faced that question in my career and am not always proud of the answer. My interactions with people in career transition tell me that the majority wrestle with this problem as well.

Ideas for Achieving Balance

◊ We spend most of our lives at work, but it shouldn't consume most of our lives. Be more intentional in your next job. Make different priorities that will help you achieve balance. For example: (a) be home for dinner every night, (b) have a new "show-up agenda" and attend the kid's activities, (c) make time for me—exercise, reading, friends, and (d) make date nights and better communication with my spouse a priority.

◊ Ask your family and friends to hold you accountable in your pursuit of balance. Get feedback on a frequent basis on how you are doing with balance.

◊ Ask yourself from time to time if your work is serving your family and a higher purpose or is it the other way around. It is easy to get lost in the day-to-day, so course corrections will be needed.

To conclude, I realize I haven't addressed every challenge job seekers face today, nor was that the intent. I simply wanted to share what I have learned from others who may be in similar situations and address the issues they are struggling with both personally and professionally. I encourage us to at least consider the positives that can come from all this and look at new ways to overcome these difficult times.

Our jobs place enormous demands on our time and will consume us if we are not careful. But good things can come of it. Dean Harbry, executive coach and founder of Internal Innovations, offers: "I have observed a common thread with my displaced clients. They are asking the question, 'What is my purpose, and how can I find a way to live that purpose in my next job?' Times of transition can be more helpful than you realize as you spend time with family, dig deep on what truly motivates you, and validate that notion through the feedback of those around you. Your spouse, children, and close friends have a superior vantage point to help you make the next step into more meaningful work."

As you pursue the next job in your career, think about these lessons and be more intentional about staying relevant, seeking healthier validation, and leading a more balanced life. Self-discovery can be a little scary, but I hope what I have shared in this appendix will inspire you and prepare you for the next phase of your life journey. We all need to make a living, but we need to live while we are working. We would all love a second chance to "get it right." Maybe this is yours.

Other books by Randy Hain

Along the Way: Lessons for an Authentic Journey of Faith
Foreword by Tom Peterson
Liguori Publications (2012)
ISBN: 978-0-7648-2164-6

The Catholic Briefcase: Tools for Integrating Faith and Work
Foreword by Patrick Lencioni
Liguori Publications (2011)
ISBN: 978-0-7648-2052-6

Available at bookstores, Amazon, and Liguori.org.